# AS/A-LEVEL YEAR 1
## STUDENT GUIDE

## WJEC/Eduqas

# Business

## Business opportunities

Mark Hage

Tracey Bell

**HODDER**
EDUCATION
AN HACHETTE UK COMPANY

Hodder Education, an Hachette UK company, Blenheim Court, George Street, Banbury, Oxfordshire OX16 5BH

### Orders

Bookpoint Ltd, 130 Park Drive, Milton Park, Abingdon, Oxfordshire OX14 4SB

tel: 01235 827720

fax: 01235 400401

e-mail: education@bookpoint.co.uk

Lines are open 9.00 a.m.–5.00 p.m., Monday to Saturday, with a 24-hour message answering service. You can also order through the Hodder Education website: www.hoddereducation.co.uk

ISBN 978-1-5104-1986-5

First printed 2018

Impression number 8 7 6 5

Year 2022 2021 2020

This Guide has been written specifically to support students preparing for the WJEC/Eduqas AS and A-level Business examinations. The content has been neither approved nor endorsed by WJEC/Eduqas and remains the sole responsibility of the authors.

Cover photograph: Sashkin/Shutterstock

Typeset by Integra Software Services Pvt. Ltd., Pondicherry, India

Printed in Dubai

Hachette UK's policy is to use papers that are natural, renewable and recyclable products and made from wood grown in sustainable forests. The logging and manufacturing processes are expected to conform to the environmental regulations of the country of origin.

# Contents

# ■Getting the most from this book

## Exam tips

Advice on key points in the text to help you learn and recall content, avoid pitfalls, and polish your exam technique in order to boost your grade.

## Knowledge check

Rapid-fire questions throughout the Content Guidance section to check your understanding.

## Knowledge check answers

1 Turn to the back of the book for the Knowledge check answers.

## Summaries

■ Each core topic is rounded off by a bullet-list summary for quick-check reference of what you need to know.

Questions & Answers

## 1 WJEC AS

### Extract 1

The milk market is worth £2 billion per year in the UK (June 2011). Milk is sold in cheap, clear plastic containers in litres at supermarkets, such as Tesco or Aldi. Typically little attention is paid to the packaging other than the name and type of milk. One litre of milk typically sells for £0.75 across most shops and has a shelf life of 2–3 days.

Cravendale is a highly successful niche brand of milk launched by UK company Arla in 2004. It uses a special type of filtering to remove more impurities from the milk than ordinary milk. Together with white plastic bottles and labels that stand out the milk has a shelf life of up to 3 weeks. Cravendale has a sophisticated marketing campaign using television adverts and social media to raise awareness of its product, spending £5 million on advertising per year. Cravendale is sold in supermarkets at a premium price of £1.15 per litre. Arla posted profits of £8.3 million in 2012.

Tesco has now launched its own brand of filtered milk at the lower price of £0.95 per litre.

Niche markets

**Briefly explain two drawbacks of operating in a niche market.**                     (4 marks)

ⓔ 'Briefly explain' means you need to identify drawbacks and how they link to the business, justifying your answer.

Understanding: identify a drawback of operating in a niche market (AO1). This is worth up to 2 marks.

Analysis: understand the impact on the business of each drawback (AO3). This is worth up to 2 marks.

### Student A

A niche market is part of a mass market 🔲 Cravendale milk is a niche market product. 🔲

One disadvantage of Cravendale operating in a niche market is with fewer potential customers compared to a mass market product costs in making the product will be higher. 🔲

ⓔ 2/4 marks awarded. 🔲The student has mistakenly tried to gain a mark by providing a definition of niche market, even though no marks are available for this. 🔲Although the student used the name 'Cravendale' this is simply restating what the extract text states so gains no mark. 🔲The student gives an accurate drawback for a business that operates in a niche market and so scores 1 AO1 mark. This is briefly developed to gain 1 AO3 mark.

**Exam-style questions**

**Commentary on the questions**

Tips on what you need to do to gain full marks, indicated by the icon ⓔ

**Sample student answers**

Practise the questions, then look at the student answers that follow.

**Commentary on sample student answers**

Read the comments (preceded by the icon ⓔ) showing how many marks each answer would be awarded in the exam and exactly where marks are gained or lost.

# ■ About this book

This guide (Student Guide 1) has been written with one goal in mind: to provide you with the ideal resource for your revision of both the WJEC/Eduqas Business AS and the first year of the WJEC/Eduqas Business A-level.

In your study of the subject you will look at business in a variety of contexts, small and large, national and global, service and manufacturing. This book covers the theme of Unit/Component 1: Business opportunities.

The **Content Guidance** section offers concise coverage of Unit/Component 1, combining an overview of key terms and concepts with identification of opportunities for you to illustrate the higher-level skills of analysis and evaluation.

The **Questions & Answers** section provides examples of stimulus materials and the various types of questions that you are likely to face: both short-answer and data-response questions. The questions cover both WJEC AS and WJEC Eduqas AS and A-level Business. They also give explanations of command words which can be applied to any question with the same word. The answers are also explained in detail, including the grades obtained.

A common problem for students and teachers is the lack of resources and in particular exam-style questions that cover individual areas of study. The questions in this guide are tailored so you can apply your learning while the topic is still fresh in your mind, either during the course itself or when you have revised a topic in preparation for the examination. Along with the sample answers this should provide you with a sound basis for sitting your exams in Business.

## Pre-existing knowledge

AS and A-level Business presumes you have no specific previous experience of the subject and its key terms. The good news is that everyone starts at the very beginning as regards the key terms and knowledge. The most important existing attribute at this stage is an interest in the current news in terms of businesses you are familiar with, such as Apple and McDonald's. Business is a subject that requires you to apply key terms to real businesses so an interest in businesses in the news will help you to contextualise the theories. It is the really enjoyable part of the subject, and allows you ultimately to score highly in the exam.

# Content Guidance

## ▮ Enterprise

### Enterprise and small to medium-sized enterprises (SMEs)

**Enterprise** is what a person uses when running a business. It includes initiative and risk taking, such as that taken by Nancy's Nails when selling scented nail polish.

**Small to medium-sized enterprises** (SMEs) are businesses whose personnel numbers fall below certain limits. In 2016, there were 5.5 million businesses in the UK of which 99.3% were SMEs. SMEs employed 15.7 million people in 2016, amounting to 60% of all private sector employment in the UK. The amount of sales in 2016 for SMEs in the UK was £1.8 trillion or 47% of all private sector sales recorded.

**Knowledge check 1**

Give one reason why SMEs made up 99.3% of all UK businesses in 2016.

### The role of the entrepreneur in business opportunities

An **entrepreneur** is someone who takes a risk by starting an enterprise known commonly as a business. An entrepreneur:

- Provides goods and services that customers want or need. A **need** is something a human cannot live without such as food or clothing. A **want** is something a human desires such as designer clothes rather than cheaper clothes from Primark.
- Creates and sets up a business, which involves having a business idea and the financial capital to make this idea a reality. The idea may come from observation that a key service is lacking locally, or may be the result of a scientific or technical study that leads to a new invention or innovation.

Further development is often done through a business plan, which is a forecast of business operations, including a cash-flow forecast/statement of business objectives and a plan of staffing needs or marketing methods.

**Knowledge check 2**

Give a reason why Richard Branson is such a successful entrepreneur.

Innovation within a business will come not only from the entrepreneur but also through employees and other people linked to the business.

This may lead to the creation of new parts of the business or even new businesses. In a business such as the Dyson company, innovation is encouraged by giving design engineers the time to develop their own product ideas. These can then form part of a wave of new product development for the company, to the benefit of all staff.

**Good** A physical product, such as a car.

**Service** An intangible product (i.e. you cannot touch it), such as financial advice or a bus journey.

**Business plan** Set of documents prepared by a firm's management to summarise its operational and financial objectives for the near future.

**Innovation** The process of translating an idea or invention into a good or service that creates value for which customers will pay.

# Entrepreneurial motives and characteristics

## Entrepreneurial motives

Entrepreneurial motives are the reasons that drive a person or people to set up in business. These include financial motives such as making a profit or making the maximum profit available, known as **profit maximisation**.

**Non-profit motives** include:

- **Satisficing** — the motive is to make sufficient profits to satisfy the entrepreneur but not necessarily the greatest profit possible.
- **Ethical stance** — starting a business with the intention of helping others, e.g. producing more comfortable wheelchairs for people with disabilities.
- **Social entrepreneurship** — the motive is to create a sustainable, profit-making business that also benefits the community, e.g. a second-hand bookshop.
- **Independence and home working** —the entrepreneur wants more freedom to work when and where they please, perhaps to fit around family or other commitments.

## Entrepreneurial characteristics

Entrepreneurial characteristics are personality traits and skills that an entrepreneur needs to have in order to start and run a successful business. The main characteristics are a risk-taking attitude, creativity, resilience (being able to cope with setbacks), self-confidence and determination.

# The importance and impact of entrepreneurs and SMEs on the UK economy

Entrepreneurs and SMEs are important to the UK economy because:

- SMEs and entrepreneurs have combined sales of £1.8 trillion which accounted for 47% of all business sales in 2016.
- They generate a large amount of direct employment — 15.7 million jobs in the UK in 2016 — and indirect employment through the goods and services such businesses purchase. SMEs accounted for 60% of all private sector jobs in 2016.
- Many SMEs offer innovative products and services and often grow significantly quicker than established larger businesses. Growth means more jobs and wealth creation for the economy and is vital to the sustainable success of a country. For example, Facebook launched in the UK in 2006 with 1 million users in its first year and had got 32 million users by 2016.

Entrepreneurial motives The reasons that drive a person or people to set up in business.

**Knowledge check 3**

Why might the ethical motives of Anita Roddick, the founder of The Body Shop, have been a key factor in the success of her natural beauty product business?

**Exam tip**

Make sure you do not confuse entrepreneurial motives and characteristics.

Entrepreneurial characteristics Personality traits and skills that an entrepreneur needs to have in order to start and run a successful business.

**Exam tip**

You will need to identify and evaluate the importance of specific characteristics from the stimulus material.

**Knowledge check 5**

Give one reason why SMEs may find it difficult to start up in car manufacturing.

- The largest industries in the UK are retail, manufacturing and vehicle repairs. SMEs account for 46% of these businesses. SMEs make up a large proportion of the **primary sector**, which are organisations that are at the first stage of production, such as farms and fishing. SMEs also make up a considerable proportion of the **secondary sector**, which is the second stage of the production process using primary resources and converting them into products, e.g. car manufacturers. Finally, SMEs make up a large proportion of the final stage of production which is the **tertiary sector**. The tertiary sector provides services such as retailing and restaurants.

# The various stakeholders who are affected by a business

A **stakeholder** is a person, group or organisation that has an interest or concern in a business. Stakeholders include shareholders, employees, managers, suppliers, lenders and the community in which the business operates.

**Internal stakeholders** are groups within a business, for example, owners, workers and shareholders. **External stakeholders** are groups outside a business, for example, the community, suppliers, customers and lenders.

Figure 1 shows examples of the internal and external stakeholders for a company.

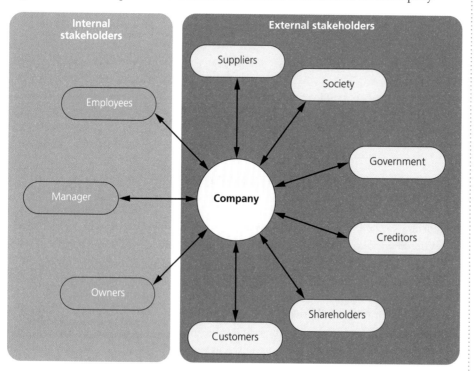

**Figure 1** Internal and external stakeholders

Table 1 shows the main impacts of a business for different stakeholders, listing the positive effects a business may have on each. Negative effects will be the opposite of those listed.

**Table 1** How a business affects the main stakeholder groups

| Stakeholder group | Business effect |
|---|---|
| Staff | Growth: new technology by product, not process, means greater production and more jobs; rising profits mean rising wages (particularly if they are shared with staff). |
| Managers/ directors | Growth: new technology by process or product means a more efficient and productive business; rising profits (especially if bonuses are available) mean greater pay. |
| Shareholders | Rising profits, short term and long term, mean greater payments for investment and more valuable shares. Falling profits risk the opposite. |
| Suppliers | Growth means more orders and greater profits. |
| Customers | Quality of product and service: innovative new products and improving customer service mean a better customer experience and reliability from products. |
| Banks | Stable profits mean the business is able to pay back any current loans and be seen as a lower risk for any future finance required, e.g. for expansion. |
| Local residents | Clean, green production with few deliveries or despatches means the local community has a positive view of the business, making expansion easier. |

**Knowledge check 7**

What might employees ask for when a business has steadily climbing profits?

## Summary

After studying this topic, you should be able to:
- explain the meaning and importance of enterprise, entrepreneurs and SMEs
- identify business opportunities and how satisfying wants and needs can give opportunities to entrepreneurs
- explain the financial and non-financial motives of entrepreneurs and the characteristics and skills that can make them successful
- explain the importance of entrepreneurs and SMEs to the primary, secondary and tertiary sectors of the UK economy
- evaluate the impact of entrepreneurs and SMEs on businesses and the economy
- identify the various stakeholders who are affected by a business

# ■ Business plans

## The purpose and main components of a business plan

A **business plan** is a forecast of business operations, including a cash-flow forecast/statement of business objectives and a plan of staffing needs and marketing methods. A business plan will include:

- **A marketing plan**, which will include market research such as market mapping of key competitors and their products together with a medium–long term plan for achieving objectives such as higher market share or a stronger product portfolio.
- **An operational plan** showing how the product will be produced and delivered to customers in its target market.
- **A financial plan** with a prediction of the business's income from sales and expenditure from costs over a period of time. This will help the business to assess its short-, medium- and long-term needs in terms of finance.
- **A human resources plan**, which will predict the staff needs of the business, including the level of skills and numbers of staff needed to achieve the business objectives. This plan will include predictions of staff turnover and managers required to supervise employees.
- **An executive plan,** which is a short summary of the main points from the detailed plan, such as key objectives of the business, key staff and financial information, e.g. revenue and profit for the next five years.

> **Business plan** A forecast of business operations, including a statement of business objectives, a cash-flow forecast, a plan of staffing needs and marketing methods.

## The importance and purpose of a business plan

A business plan is an important document:

- For investors and lenders of finance because they will want to see detailed **forecasts** of how the business will perform over time. The forecast includes predictions of sales, expenditure, income and profit.
- To obtain finance there must also be evidence of an analysis of the market and that there are sufficient skills and commitment to meet the forecasts in the business plan. Lenders and investors will then be able to assess the risks of their potential investment in terms of the ability of the business to pay it back.
- The benefit to the business is that reducing the risks to investors means they may be able to pay lower interest rates on loans or give smaller shares of the business to venture capitalists, keeping costs to a minimum while keeping as much ownership and control of the business as possible.
- A business plan helps the business to look logically and methodically at the steps needed to achieve its aims and objectives, e.g. from drawing a new design for a car to putting it into production and generating sufficient sales to make a profit.
- A plan can then be compared to actual progress to see whether deadlines, costs and profits are as predicted.
- All parts of the business can measure their performance in achieving the plan and any problems can be identified and addressed before any major ones occur.

> **Forecast** A calculation or estimate of how the business will perform in future in terms of financial and other measurements of success.

> **Knowledge check 8**
>
> Name one reason why a business plan may not help a business to be successful.

However, a plan by itself is of little use to a business. The biggest mistake made regarding business plans is they are not realistic and therefore fail to be followed.

The best business plans are those that are living documents which are regularly amended to allow for unexpected problems such as changes in costs or significantly more demand than can be produced. For example, the Nintendo Switch games console was initially planned for a production run of 8 million in 2017. However, due to unexpectedly high demand Nintendo has had to double production with its suppliers now planning to produce 16 million units in 2017. Clearly Nintendo had a sufficiently flexible business plan to allow for this massive increase in production.

## The main sources of information and guidance available to entrepreneurs

The main sources of information and guidance available to entrepreneurs are:

- Government organisations such as GOV.UK, Business Wales and the Department for Business, Energy and Industrial strategy. All offer free advice through website and/or courses to entrepreneurs on a range of issues from the legal requirements for setting up a business to workshops on how to create a business plan. Governments are keen to support new entrepreneurs, called 'start-ups', as they understand that the SMEs of today may become the Dysons of tomorrow, generating wealth for the whole economy.
- Government organisations also offer grants for new businesses, which are non-repayable, and loans, which must be repaid. For example, SMEs can apply for innovation grants in 2017. These can be applied for where businesses have a new idea such as manufacturing products out of new materials, such as Graphene. Often the entrepreneur will need to match the amount of grant obtained with their own funding.
- There are many other privately-run organisations that support businesses such as the Federation of Small Businesses, the British Chamber of Commerce, Antur Teifi in Wales and various banks and financial institutions. Advice is often free with some emphasising networking and training and others offering free services that lead to paid ones, such as banks offering help with writing business plans, which can assist with a loan application.

**Knowledge check 9**

Give one reason why governments may offer businesses grants to set up in some areas but not in others.

**Summary**

After studying this topic, you should be able to:
- explain the purpose and main components of a business plan
- evaluate the importance of a business plan
- identify the main sources of information and guidance available to entrepreneurs

# Markets

A **product** is a physical product, such as a car. A **service** is an intangible product (i.e. you cannot touch it), such as financial advice or a bus journey. Businesses sell either products or services to customers.

A **customer** is someone who buys a product from a business. Customers can include end users of the product. **Trade customers** are businesses who sell the product or an enhanced version of it to customers. For example, a carpenter may buy wood from a timber merchant and then sell wardrobes that have been made from this wood to customers at a significant profit.

A **consumer** is someone who uses goods and services produced by businesses. For example, you may purchase a bottle of Coca-Cola as a customer and then give this to your friend to drink, who would be the consumer.

A **market** refers to a place where buyers and sellers trade goods and services with each other. Markets can be physical, such as a supermarket or a town centre with shops. Increasingly, many markets are also based online such as car insurance, the purchase of electronic goods and even the weekly grocery shop.

**Competition** is where two or more sellers of similar goods or services act independently to persuade buyers to choose their products. In some markets, competition is fierce, such as the car insurance market. In other markets, there are few competitors so there is little rivalry. For example, there are many companies that provide water, but in the UK only one company currently operates in each geographical area (e.g. United Utilities covers the northwest of England). The rise of the internet and easy comparison of prices and services have revolutionised competition in some markets (e.g. purchasing a television can include looking at prices across physical and internet stores to find the best deal).

## Different types of market

### Local and global markets

A **local market** is where customers only travel a short distance to purchase goods or services from sellers. For example, shopping for groceries, getting your hair cut or having a meal at a restaurant. Local markets are easy to access but are normally relatively small.

A **global market** is where goods and services are offered for sale by businesses across different countries. For example, oil is bought and sold across most countries dependent on the price through multinational companies such as BP and Shell. With the increasing use of the internet physical borders to buying and selling products are becoming less important, particularly for businesses that trade in electronic items. For example, streaming media services such as Amazon Prime, Netflix and Spotify compete with each other.

A **seasonal market** is one where sales are concentrated in a particular part of the year rather than being spread throughout the year. For example, sales of Christmas trees occur almost exclusively in December.

---

**Knowledge check 10**

Name one reason why Nintendo may target its advertising at consumers of the new Switch games console rather than customers.

**Market** A place where buyers and sellers trade goods and services with each other.

**Competition** Two or more sellers of similar goods or services act independently to persuade buyers to choose their products.

**Knowledge check 11**

Why might a water company be able to charge customers more for their water supply even when its costs are decreasing?

# Mass market

Mass market refers to a large market of customers with widely different backgrounds that a business will not try to distinguish between. It is said to be **undifferentiated**.

An example of a mass market is the selling of milk in supermarkets. Milk is sold in many different shops with the product varying little in quality or looks, therefore being undifferentiated.

Advantages of operating in a mass market include being able to purchase goods and materials in bulk, known as **economies of scale**. Dealing with high sales volumes makes it easier to afford large advertising and marketing campaigns.

The disadvantage to being in a mass market is that the competition is likely to be fierce as businesses are attracted to potentially high sales levels. To stand out from the crowd a **unique selling point** is hugely helpful, for example, Bounty, the only chocolate bar filled with coconut.

# Niche market

A niche market is the smaller section of a larger market on which a product or service is focused. It is aimed at satisfying specific market needs by creating a carefully tailored product.

An example of a niche market would be specialised milk such as filtered milk, which is a smaller section of the milk market. Not all shops sell filtered milk, so it is uncommon in terms of its availability. In addition, it is aimed at meeting different customer needs, those of customers who want a product that is perceived as being of a higher quality than ordinary milk.

The advantages of a business being in a niche market are that there is less competition from other businesses and products can be tailored to meet customers' needs.

The disadvantage of a business being in a niche market is that as this is a smaller part of the larger market there are fewer potential customers, therefore it may be difficult to persuade retailers to stock the product(s).

## Differences between niche and mass market
- A niche market is small, but focused on one specific type of customer.
- A mass market product may have a lower price than a niche market product.
- Identifying a new niche market is a classic way in which new small firms can find a profitable niche for themselves.

# Trade and consumer markets

A trade market is where a business is selling to another business rather than an ordinary householder (e.g. JCB selling a digger to a construction company). In trade markets, branding tends to be relatively unimportant — business buyers want high quality products at good prices. Therefore pricing and other strategies have to be tailored to the business buyer's needs. This type of market is known as business to business or B2B.

Mass market A large market of customers which is undifferentiated and that sells products and services to suit a large number of people.

**Exam tip**

Accurate definitions are the key to a good mark when answering exam questions. If they are both precise and concise, it will save you time in the exam room.

**Knowledge check 12**

Give one benefit of a global business designing different products for different countries.

Niche market A smaller part of a large market, with products tailored to specific customer needs.

**Knowledge check 13**

Lindor chocolate was once in a tiny, luxury niche; now it is a mass market brand. What benefits may brand-owner Lindt gain from this?

Trade market Where a business is selling to another business rather than an ordinary householder.

A consumer market is where a business is selling a product to the general public. The emphasis for the business is on branding and image — though of course customers want well-designed, well-made products too. The buying process is focused on emotional issues and is very short. For example, an item of clothing is well understood by the customer and may be bought due to its brand, such as Chanel, and the aspirational image such products have for customers. This type of market is known as business to consumer or B2C.

## Analyse and interpret the market

**Market analysis** is the process of gathering information about anything that has or will affect conditions in the market in which a business operates. **Market data**, which are information collected by a business from different sources, can help the business to understand:

- Market size: the total value or quantity of demand in a specific market or period of time. For example, the total number of sales of cars in the UK in 2016 was 2.69 million according to the Society of Motor Manufacturers and Traders (SMMT).
- Market share: the proportion of sales a business or product has achieved expressed as a percentage in a period of time. For example, according to the SMMT the biggest selling car in 2016 was the Ford Fiesta, with a market share of 4.24%.
- Market trends: taking a series of market data over a period of time to try to predict what will happen in the future. For example, figures for new car sales in the UK in 2015 and 2016 show a trend of sales growing by 2%. However, the SMMT has predicted that this growth trend is likely to stop in 2017.

Businesses can use market data to analyse and predict future trends to inform important decisions such as whether to make more products or introduce new ones. For example, a trend in the UK car market appears to be growth in electric vehicles, with sales up 3.3% in 2016 compared to 2015. Businesses such as Ford may wish to look at taking advantage of this trend to offset any potential fall in other products.

> **Exam tip**
>
> Examiners will reward you well for identifying market trends from data provided, especially if you can give the benefits and risks to the business of relying on such trends.

## Market segmentation

Market segmentation involves dividing a market into a smaller set of customers, or segments, who have similar needs and interests. Segmenting a market can be done through different ways including by gender, age, location or income. For example, a bank might segment its potential customers into those aged 18–24 in order to look at the needs and wants of these customers in terms of offering bank accounts.

Segmentation is important to a business and its customers because:

- It allows a business to decide which segments it wants to focus on in terms of product or service.
- Marketing can be more effectively focused on a specific set of customers such as small car buyers.

---

**Consumer market** Selling a product to the general public.

> **Exam tip**
>
> You will gain the most marks by relating your analysis of markets to any stimulus material provided.

**Market size** The total value or quantity of demand in a specific market or period of time.

**Market share** The proportion of sales a business or product has achieved expressed as a percentage in a period of time.

**Market trends** Taking a series of market data over a period of time to try to predict what will happen in the future.

> **Knowledge check 14**
>
> Give one reason why market data may be unreliable in predicting trends in a market.

**Market segmentation** Dividing a market into a smaller set of customers who have similar needs and interests.

- The business can become more cost effective and efficient.
- Customers are more likely to be able to buy products or services that meet their specific needs potentially at a lower cost.

Advantages for a business using market segmentation are that it creates separate products for each segment, which means the business can focus on how best to meet those customers' needs, and it can increase sales by allowing the business to identify areas of growth for products and services. The main disadvantage with segmentation is that producing a number of products to suit different tastes is expensive — and can make it difficult for any of them to make a profit.

# Different degrees of competition

The competitive environment is how fiercely other businesses compete with the products that another business makes. The more competition there is in a market the more likely consumers will benefit, for example, businesses are likely to be more price sensitive and more market orientated.

In the supermarket sector competition became very fierce after Aldi and other discount retailers entered the market. Their arrival forced businesses such as Tesco to offer customers much better, everyday low pricing in order to maintain market share.

A market can be split into:

- **One dominant business**. This is called a monopoly which is normally said to be a business which has 25% or more of the industry's sales. An example of a business that operates a monopoly would be Apple and its iPod, which has a 70% share (by value) of the US MP3 player market.

  A monopoly business is able to restrict choices that consumers have over products and services and is often able to charge higher prices for goods than if the same product was in a competitive market. Benefits of a monopoly include economies of scale, such as being able to buy raw materials in bulk at a lower unit cost, and a faster rate of technological development due to their high profitability.

- **A few large businesses.** This is known as an oligopoly. Markets that are large have a potentially large number of customers and can support the launch of new products or services with fewer risks than smaller markets. However, as there are many potential customers this is likely to encourage more competitors who are attracted by high profits and large growth.

- Perfect competition. This is a market where buyers and businesses are so great in number and so well informed about each other that the market price cannot be controlled by any one buyer or business. Products in the market can be easily substituted and new businesses can enter and exit the market easily. An example of a market that may be close to achieving perfect competition is one that operates on the internet (e.g. sellers of books on eBay can set up easily and with little cost and buyers and sellers can see what is available and at what price). Businesses tend to set prices close to those of competitors.

  However, perfect competition is often seen as a goal rather than something which is achievable in practice. For example, most customers have imperfect information about what products are available in a market and can be influenced by marketing, and products sold by businesses often have differences that distinguish their products from competitors' ones.

---

**Knowledge check 15**

If a market segment is worth 20% of total sales and the sales for the whole market are worth £3.2 million, what is the value of the segment?

**Competitive environment** How fiercely other businesses compete with the products that another business makes.

**Monopoly** A business which has 25% or more of the industry's sales.

**Oligopoly** A market dominated by a few producers, each of which has control over the market.

**Perfect competition** A market where buyers and businesses are so great in number and so well informed about each other that the market price cannot be controlled by any one firm.

- **Monopolistic competition.** This is a market where many firms offer products that are similar but not exact substitutes, for example hairdressers and restaurants. Unlike a monopoly there are low barriers to entering or leaving the market. There are many businesses and consumers and businesses are able to have some control over price. Businesses tend to advertise a lot as products are similar though there will be differences, with businesses attempting to sell at slightly different price levels to consumers. Consumers will find it difficult to decide what is a fair price and what the exact differences are between products, for example whether Samsung's range of 'Quantum dot' televisions are as good as LG's OLED televisions.

All markets change over time, including expanding and contracting in terms of competition and potential customers. Businesses need to be able to respond to a more competitive environment by lowering prices or improving their customer service. However, a business may not have sufficient funds to sustain this approach or competitors may also cut prices. Alternatively, a business may increase its product differentiation to create a unique selling point for its product and a stronger brand image that encourages sales and customer loyalty.

# Reasons why consumers need protection from business exploitation

In situations where a market is said to have perfect competition there is little need to protect consumers from business exploitation — each business is already aware that any such action would mean a total loss of business to other competitors. However, the reality is that markets have imperfect competition, ranging from fiercely competitive markets to monopolistic markets. Reasons for protecting consumers include:

- Most businesses see profit as their main motive, which can lead to overcharging customers for unsatisfactory products or products that are not fit for purpose.
- Businesses also seek to reduce costs and this can lead to products that are unsafe and defective.
- The line between fair advertising of products and misleading or false statements about products can sometimes be difficult for businesses to comprehend. Some businesses also make false claims about their products to increase profit and sales (e.g. designer handbags that are not Louis Vuitton but are advertised as such).
- Some businesses charge a large amount of interest (profit) to give credit to customers or pressure customers into signing agreements to purchase goods they do not want (e.g. double glazing).

In order to deter businesses from exploiting consumers Parliament has passed laws, known as legislation, to make the relationship between businesses and customers fairer.

The areas of legislation that affect businesses are:

- **Consumer protection:** laws aimed at making sure that businesses act fairly towards their customers and consumers.
- **Sale and Supply of Goods Act:** this states that goods must be of satisfactory quality, for example a hairdryer must safely dry hair.

**Monopolistic competition** A market where many firms offer products that are similar but not exact substitutes, e.g. hairdressers and restaurants. Unlike a monopoly there are low barriers to entering or leaving the market.

**Knowledge check 16**

Name one way in which Apple has tried to maintain its dominant position in the tablet market.

**Exam tip**

You need to be able to identify from the extracts the environment the business is operating in *now* and relate this to how things may change *in the future*, for example through technology. You might conclude that markets are rarely static so a monopoly situation may become a fiercely competitive market over time.

**Legislation** The laws passed by Parliament in the UK or the European Union that affect business.

- **Trade Descriptions Act:** this states that goods and services must perform in the way advertised by the business, for example a car advertised as having air conditioning must have this feature.
- **Environmental protection:** going back to the Clean Air Act 1956 (which ended the infamous London 'smogs') laws to protect the environment have had a big effect on businesses. The impact on businesses can be considerable, as it may be expensive to install filtration systems that clean the smoke coming from factories. As less developed countries tend to have lower legal requirements, this might affect the international competitiveness of UK businesses. But even today air pollution kills 30,000 people a year in the UK, so not many people would try to make a case for enfeebling the UK's legal requirements.
- **Competition policy:** laws aiming to ensure that fair competition takes place in each industry. Governments believe that greater competition leads to lower prices, better quality goods and a wider variety of products. The Competitions and Markets Authority can investigate takeovers, mergers, anti-competitive practices and bring criminal proceedings against individuals who commit **cartel** offences. Any business that appears to be restricting fair competition can be investigated by the Competition and Markets Authority.

# Demand

**Demand** is the amount of a good or service which customers buy at a given price and within a given time period.

Demand is normally illustrated through the use of a demand curve diagram which has two axes. The X axis, the horizontal line running along the bottom of the diagram, represents the quantity of the goods or services being sold. The Y axis, running vertically from bottom to top of the diagram, represents the price at which the goods are sold. The line drawn is called the demand curve and each point of the demand curve represents the amount of goods or services a customer is willing to buy at that price.

## Factors leading to a change in demand

The demand for a good or service will go up if the price is cut. The demand for a good or service will go down the higher the price. Price is the only factor that moves demand up and down the demand curve. All other factors that change demand move the curve left or right of its starting position in Figure 2. This means there will be a new demand curve.

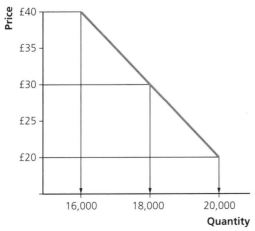

**Figure 2** Demand curve for concert tickets

**Knowledge check 17**

Name one way a business that sells mobile phones can try to minimise the impact of consumer protection legislation on its profits.

**Cartel** An association of manufacturers or suppliers formed with the purpose of maintaining prices at a high level and restricting competition.

**Demand** The amount of a good or service that customers are prepared to buy at a given price and within a given period.

**Exam tip**

You need to be able to draw a demand curve diagram and be able to explain what is happening to demand and why.

If the demand curve shifts to the left of its original position, it means demand for the product or service has decreased, as in Figure 3.

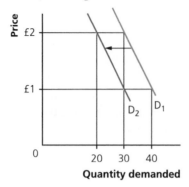

**Figure 3** Demand curve showing shift to the left

If the demand curve shifts to the right of its original position, it means demand for the product or service has increased, as in Figure 4.

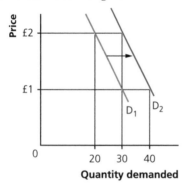

**Figure 4** Demand curve showing shift to the right

The main factors that can lead to a change in demand are:

- Changes in the prices of **substitute goods**. If the price of one good increases, then demand for the substitute is likely to rise, meaning the demand curve will shift to the right for the substitute for the good (see Figure 5).

**Substitute goods** Two goods that can be used for the same purpose, e.g. Cadbury's Dairy Milk and Galaxy chocolate.

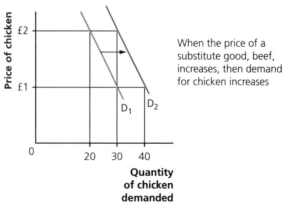

When the price of a substitute good, beef, increases, then demand for chicken increases

**Figure 5** Demand curve showing increase in demand for substitute good

- Changes in the prices of complementary goods. If the demand for one good goes up then demand for the complementary good will also rise, meaning the demand curve will shift to the right for both the good and the complementary good (see Figure 6).

**Complementary good**
One that is used together with another good, e.g. cars and petrol — if car prices fall, the demand for cars will rise, and so will demand for petrol.

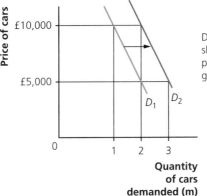

Demand curve for cars shifts to the right when the price of a complementary good, petrol, decreases

**Figure 6** Demand curve showing increase in demand for complementary good

- Changes in **consumer incomes**. If incomes increase, customers will buy more of the product or service, shifting the demand curve to the right (see Figure 7).

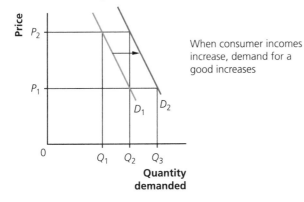

When consumer incomes increase, demand for a good increases

**Figure 7** Demand curve showing increase in demand due to increase in consumer incomes

- **Fashions, tastes and preferences**. If a business's product or service becomes more fashionable, then the demand curve will shift to the right.
- **Advertising** and branding. If a business spends heavily on advertising, the demand curve should shift to the right, meaning more demand.
- **Demographics**, such as population trends. With the number of over-65s increasing, the demand for Stannah stairlifts, for example, will rise, pushing the demand curve to the right.
- **External shocks**, such as a recession or sharp change in exchange rates. When the UK economy is in recession the demand curve for most products shifts to the left as customers struggle with less disposable income (see Figure 8).

**Branding** The process involved in creating a unique name and image for a product in the customer's mind, mainly through advertising campaigns with a consistent theme.

**Recession** A period of temporary economic decline in a country during which trade and industrial activity are reduced.

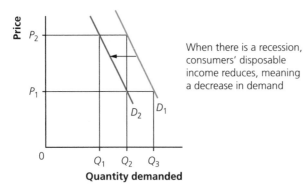

When there is a recession, consumers' disposable income reduces, meaning a decrease in demand

**Figure 8** Demand curve showing a decrease in demand due to a recession

**Exam tip**

The demand for most products is affected by more than one factor. This can make it hard to judge which is the most important. Good exam answers are bold in selecting factors and backing them with supporting argument.

- **Seasonality.** Some goods or services have a change in demand depending on the time of year they are sold. For example, the demand curve for sales of ice cream will shift to the right with increased demand in the summer.

# Supply

**Supply** is the amount of goods or services provided at a given price by all the companies within a market.

Supply is normally illustrated through the use of a supply curve diagram (see Figure 9). The diagram has two axes. The X axis represents the quantity of the goods or services being supplied. The Y axis represents the price at which the goods are supplied. Each point of the supply curve represents the amount of goods or services a business is willing to supply at that price.

**Supply** The amount of goods or services provided at a time at a given price.

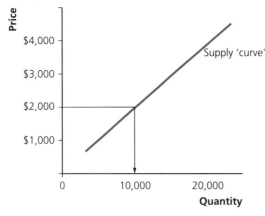

**Figure 9** A supply curve

# Factors leading to a change in supply

The supply curve slopes upwards because the higher the price, the more businesses will want to supply. A high selling price means high profits can be made by the supplier, so companies may switch resources from other production to focus on the market with high prices/profits. The supply for a good or service will go down the lower the price as businesses will be discouraged from creating more of their product as they may make less profit. Price is the only factor that moves supply up and down the supply curve.

All other factors that change supply shift the curve left or right of its starting position on the diagram. This means there will be a new supply curve.

The main factors that can lead to a change in supply are:

- Changes in the **costs of production,** where the costs of making the product from raw materials go up or down. Where the costs of production increase, the supply curve will shift left and supply will reduce.
- Introduction of **new technology** is likely to mean the business can create the product at a lower cost, encouraging greater supply. This means the supply curve will shift to the right and supply will increase (see Figure 10).

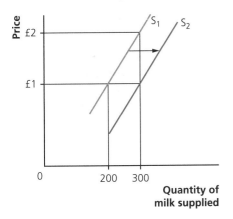

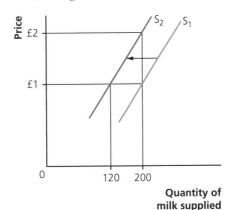

**Figure 10** Supply curve shifting to the right due to introduction of new technology

**Figure 11** Supply curve shifting to the left due to recession and increase in the cost of raw materials

- **Indirect taxes**, which are taxes of goods or services such as Value Added Tax on electricity or gas used by businesses in making or selling products or services. If indirect tax goes down the businesses will want to supply more of the product. This means the supply curve will shift to the right.
- **Government subsidies** are where the government gives money to a business to reduce its costs, normally of production. This will mean a business will supply more of the product, moving the supply curve to the right.
- **External shocks,** such as severe drought in farming areas. This will create shortages and therefore increase the cost to manufacturers of buying in raw materials. This will mean the supply curve will shift to the left (see Figure 11).

# Markets: how supply and demand affect each other

A diagram can be drawn that includes both supply and demand. The price at which the quantity demanded by customers is equal to the quantity supplied by businesses is called equilibrium (see Figure 12).

**Knowledge check 18**

Why might Ford car company increase supply if it replaces workers on its production line with robots? Explain the effect on Ford's supply curve.

**Exam tip**

Make sure to remember that the only cause of movement up and down a supply curve is a change in demand and therefore price. All other factors cause the supply curve to shift to the left (costs up) or the right (costs down).

Equilibrium The price at which the quantity demanded by customers is equal to the quantity supplied by businesses.

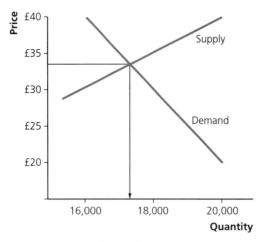

**Figure 12** Supply and demand curves for concert tickets

An example of a factor that affects supply and demand is a change in demand. For example, a rise in disposable income will result in an increase in demand. The shift in the demand curve will be to the right as demand increases, raising the equilibrium price. As a result, the supply of the product will also increase as businesses want to produce more at a higher price. So, the supply curve shifts to the right, creating a new equilibrium.

The factors that affect demand already discussed will work in the same way when considering the equilibrium of supply and demand.

A change in supply can also affect supply and demand. For example, a reduction in the costs of production, such as lower wage costs for employees, would mean the business will produce more of the product, shifting the supply curve to the right. As there is a lower price there will be greater demand and the demand curve shifts to the right, creating a new equilibrium (see Figure 13).

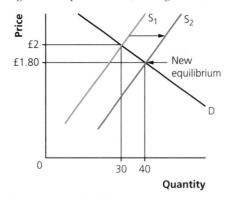

**Figure 13** Supply and demand shifting right due to lowering costs of production

# Price elasticity of demand (PED)

Price elasticity of demand measures the responsiveness of demand to a change in price.

If a company's costs have risen, it naturally wants to push up its prices to compensate. But what would be the effect on customers? If prices were increased by 5%, would sales volumes fall by 1%, 5% or perhaps even 10%? Knowing the answer to this question is vital because it determines whether the 5% price rise boosts or actually diminishes the company's revenue. If a business is selling 1,000 units a week at £20 each, and then decides to increase its price by £1 (5%), the effect would be as shown in Table 2.

**Table 2** The effects on revenue of a 5% increase in price

|  | Sales fall by 1% | Sales fall by 5% | Sales fall by 10% |
|---|---|---|---|
| New sales volume | 990 units | 950 units | 900 units |
| New price | £21 | £21 | £21 |
| New sales revenue | £20,790 | £19,950 | £18,900 |
| Change in revenue (compared with £20,000) | +£790 | −£50 | −£1,100 |

So, the effect on revenue of a 5% price rise depends on the price sensitivity of the product. If it is very price sensitive (sales fall by 10% when price rises by 5%) the price rise is self-defeating — it cuts revenue. In business, the term given for price sensitivity is price elasticity. If customers are mainly making their purchasing decisions on the basis of price, the price sensitivity/elasticity will be high. For a company, that is not good. If your products are highly price elastic, cost increases cannot easily be passed on to customers, so profits can easily be squeezed — and perhaps turn into losses.

It is important for a business to look at the amount of good or service sold compared to the price it charges.

For example, a business is looking at reducing its price to customers from £60 to £40. Sales are currently 15,000 but are predicted to reach 25,000 with the reduction in the price. As demand rises in greater proportion to the change in sale price we can conclude it is very sensitive to the price of the product — demand is elastic.

## Interpretation of the values of price elasticity of demand

The values the calculation for price income elasticity of demand shows give a business an indication of how sensitive a product is to changes in price. The values are:

- **If PED is between 0 and −1.** This means price elasticity is low, probably because it is a well-differentiated, perhaps well-branded product. Demand is price inelastic.
- **If PED = −1.** This means the percentage change in demand is exactly the same as the percentage change in price. The percentage rise in price of the product would lead to exactly the same percentage fall in demand, leaving total revenue the same.
- **If PED= −1 or more.** This means demand is very sensitive to the price of the product: demand is price elastic. This must be an undifferentiated product, such as apples at a street market. If the price of the product went up 10% demand might fall by 20%.

## Factors influencing price elasticity of demand

- The number of close substitutes. The closer substitutes there are in the market, the more elastic is demand as customers find it easier to switch to another product.
- The cost of switching between products. If there are costs involved in switching to another product, then demand is more likely to be inelastic.

**Exam tip**

You are not required to be able to do the calculation for price income elasticity of demand. However, you do need to understand what factors can affect PED.

**Exam tip**

When reading the examiner's text, think about whether the featured product/brand is price elastic or inelastic. Then use that insight to analyse how a business should set about pricing and promoting its product.

- Whether the product is a luxury or essential to the customer. Necessities tend to have an inelastic demand but luxury products tend to have a more elastic demand.
- If the product is one that customers consume out of habit. As customers become used to buying a product they become less sensitive to its price. This means the demand becomes more price inelastic and less sensitive to price increases.

## The significance of PED to a business

PED is important to a business as it helps it decide how consumers will react to a change in a product's price. If the product is sensitive to price the business can decide to:

- Cut costs instead of raising prices. This will mean more potential profit without disturbing demand.
- Cut the price to give a sharp boost to demand. This will increase revenue and may boost profit, especially if unit costs can be reduced by bulk buying.
- Attempt to make the product more price inelastic. For example, use advertising and branding to make the product more desirable to the customer or add value to the product by adding new features to make it unique, i.e. give the product a competitive advantage. For example, smartphones have moved from being a luxury to being perceived as a necessity, with leading phones like the iPhone commanding very high prices while still attracting large demand (price inelastic).

# Income elasticity of demand (YED)

Income elasticity of demand measures the responsiveness of demand to a change in households' real income.

To measure YED a formula is used which is percentage change in quantity demanded divided by the percentage change in income.

## Interpretation of the values of income elasticity of demand

- **Normal goods** have a **positive income elasticity of demand**. As a customer's income rises, more is demanded at each price. For example, if people are 3% better off they tend to buy 3% more chocolate, giving chocolate an income elasticity of +1.
- **Luxury goods and services** have an income elasticity of demand of more than +1. This means that as people become better off, they buy lots more of these products, e.g. foreign holidays.
- **Inferior goods have a negative income elasticity of demand**, meaning that demand falls as income rises. For example, a negative figure may be associated with value chocolate in a supermarket as it is relatively cheap and when consumer incomes increase the demand for this product will also decrease. This means value chocolate is likely to be an inferior good. As income elasticity is likely to be negative, demand will reduce when income rises as consumers will prefer to buy branded chocolate, which is seen as more of a luxury.

**Knowledge check 19**

What is an advantage to a business such as Apple of an inelastic good?

**Exam tip**

Beware of confusing price and income elasticity. And remember that there is no such thing as 'a product's elasticity'; an income elastic product can be price inelastic.

Income elasticity of demand = percentage change in quantity demanded/percentage change in income.

**Exam tip**

Income elasticity can be used to judge how severely a business would be affected by economic change — and is a fundamental part of any sales forecasting. Unfortunately, many students fail to see how valuable it is for answering questions.

# Factors influencing income elasticity of demand

The factors influencing income elasticity of demand are:

- The degree of attractiveness of the product to the consumer. If an iPhone 7 is an absolute must, people will be determined to get it even if their incomes are being squeezed. So even though, objectively, an iPhone is a luxury, people's desires and brand loyalty may make it more of a necessity (with a low, positive income elasticity)
- How large a proportion of household income is spent on the item. For most people a new car is a major purchase that takes a big chunk out of the household budget. By contrast, spending on TV streaming services is a small proportion. So, spending on TV streaming services is likely to be affected little by economic ups and downs. It will have a positive income elasticity, but at a low level (under +1). By contrast a new car will be a luxury good, with a figure above +1.

## The significance of income elasticity of demand (YED) to a business

YED is important as it helps managers decide how sensitive their product is in terms of demand when income changes. They can use that information to forecast sales. If, in 2017, the Chinese economy grows by 7%, sales of the Land Rover Evoque may grow by 28% because the Evoque has an income elasticity estimated at +4.

If a company's main product is a highly income-elastic luxury brand, the business can decide to:

- Focus new product development on a value-for-money brand that will appeal to people feeling under financial pressure. Then if sales of the luxury brand flag in a recession there will still be strong sales from the 'inferior', value-for-money version.
- Keep focused purely on the luxury sector, but be more cautious on the financial side, e.g. keeping an extra-strong cash-flow position to cope with downturns in sales.

## Exam tip

Do not wait to be asked about a topic such as income elasticity. If you can use it to construct an argument that is relevant to the question, then do so.

## Knowledge check 20

Give an example of a normal good.

## Summary

After studying this topic, you should be able to:

- explain what is meant by a market and competition and identify the different types of market
- analyse and interpret market data
- explain what is meant by market segmentation and how markets are segmented
- evaluate the importance and impact of segmentation to a business and its customers
- understand the different markets and degrees of competition, including perfect and monopolistic competition and their impact on business behaviour
- understand the reasons why consumers need protections from exploitation from businesses
- explain what is meant by demand, supply and equilibrium and their importance
- explain the factors that can lead to a change in demand and supply and how a change in price can impact on price and quantity
- construct and interpret demand and supply diagrams
- analyse and evaluate factors which affect demand, supply and equilibrium
- understand price and income elasticity of demand and the nature of inferior, normal and luxury goods

# ■ Market research

Market research involves gathering information about customers' attitudes, behaviour and wants in relation to a product or service. Businesses often complete market research before entering a new market and at various times while operating in a market. For example, market research can check whether customer loyalty is being maintained or is starting to slip — and how best to tackle any slippage.

The value of market research is highlighted in Figure 14 and includes:

■ Better communication between the business and customers, helping to identify who it should be talking to and what they want the most.

■ Helping to identify opportunities and what competition there is. For example, is the business missing something it can profit from?

■ Minimising risk through understanding customer needs, allowing thorough preparation to meet those needs and being able to manage costs effectively.

■ Creating benchmarks to help measure business progress. For example, how are sales doing compared to those forecasted because of market research or how do customers rate the product compared to their initial expectations?

**Market research**
Information is gathered on customers — their attitudes, behaviour and wants — in relation to a product or service.

**Figure 14** The value of market research

## Issues involved in selecting the most appropriate method of market research

Issues a business will need to consider when selecting the most appropriate method of market research include:

■ **Cost.** Primary market research is often more costly than secondary market research.

■ **Accuracy.** Using primary market research and quantitative methods can lead to more reliable and less biased results than secondary market research which has often been created for a different purpose.

■ **Objective of market research.** Primary market research will allow a more personal interaction with customers which can help companies understand issues over current or future products.

■ **Level of business expertise.** This may be insufficient to carry out reliable and unbiased research which may necessitate either hiring a company such as Gallop or using secondary market research which has been reliably prepared.

■ **Time.** A business may need to complete the market research quickly before a competitor launches a similar product.

Start-up businesses often have little money to invest in market research and therefore have to take the risk of continuing with little background information.

> **Exam tip**
>
> Remember that some of the biggest businesses in the world started off with unique ideas with little or no market research. A good evaluative point to make is that while some businesses are spending time and money on market research others have already taken the risk and placed their product in the market.

# Differences between primary and secondary market research

Table 3 outlines the key differences between primary and secondary market research.

**Table 3** Differences between primary and secondary market research

| Primary market research | Secondary market research |
| --- | --- |
| Conducted to gather first-hand information | Involves the use of information that has already been gathered for another purpose, i.e. second-hand information |
| Based on raw data | The information has already been analysed and interpreted, though possibly not in a way that is most useful to the business |
| Carried out by the business or an organisation employed by the business | Someone other than the business has already carried out the research |
| The data gathered meet the specific needs of the business | The data that have already been gathered are less likely to meet the specific needs of the business |
| Costs to the business are comparatively high as is the time taken to complete the research, e.g. having to pay staff to ask members of the public questions and collect responses | Costs to the business are comparatively low and the time taken to gather the research is short, e.g. gathering of responses from members of the public will already have taken place |

# Evaluation of the use of market research to a business and its stakeholders

Table 4 outlines the main advantages and disadvantages of using market research.

**Table 4** Advantages and disadvantages of using market research

| Advantages of market research | Disadvantages of market research |
| --- | --- |
| Using primary research in particular means a business can engage with potential customers and gain an insight into their needs which gives it an advantage over competitors. | Gathering and processing the data can be expensive and the business may lack the expertise required to gather primary data, which risks leading to false conclusions and poor decisions. |
| If businesses can build market research into their selling process not only do customers feel more involved in the process but the business can gather data that are very up to date and make adjustments to ensure that it is continuously meeting customer needs, e.g. online surveys for products or services. | There is a difficult balance between the business wishing to make quick decisions to gain an advantage over competitors and the need to get detailed information from customers. |
| Accurate and reliable data can help businesses make decisions that are less costly and risky while identifying any problems with the product or service it offers in advance. | Data collected may be biased and unreliable or they could have been gathered in a way that leads to unreliable information. This can lead to businesses making costly mistakes based on the research. |
| Businesses that operate online often gain customer agreement to the collection of data for research when signing up to a service such as Amazon or Netflix. This reduces the effect of legal and ethical issues in gathering and doing market research. | There may be legal and ethical issues with gathering the data. For example, the Data Protection Act 1998 makes it a crime to use a person's information without their consent. |

# Differences between qualitative and quantitative data

Primary and secondary market research can involve the collection of two types of data:

- **Quantitative data** involve the use of numbers such as the size of the market, the growth of the market or the number of customers a business has, e.g. the number of 50-year-old men who have taken up cycling in the last 12 months.
- **Qualitative data** look at views and opinions, but do not provide statistically reliable information, e.g. asking cyclists how comfortable a new design of top is to wear.

Table 5 outlines some of the key differences between quantitative and qualitative data.

**Table 5** Differences between quantitative and qualitative data

| Quantitative data | Qualitative data |
|---|---|
| Data that can be measured and expressed numerically | Data that capture subjects' views and opinions |
| The data are conclusive and objective, e.g. 90% of 16–24-year-olds owned a smartphone in 2016 | The data explore perceptions of issues subjectively with no conclusive outcome |
| Data are statistical and structured | Data are not statistical and are unstructured |
| Data are collected on how many or how much | Data are collected on why, e.g. why do so many 16–24-year-olds own a smartphone? |
| Sample sizes are large and representative to help recommend final course of action | Small number of non-representative sample to help develop understanding of the issues |

# Explanation and evaluation of different methods of primary and secondary research

Primary and secondary market research are the two ways in which a business can undertake market research. They are essential for any business aiming to meet the needs of its chosen market. They allow the business to gather data on customer desires in relation to a product or service and can help in forecasting potential customer demand.

## Primary market research

Primary market research gathers data first-hand, such as customer interviews, probably using specifically designed questionnaires and is carried out for a specific business.

Primary market research can be undertaken in many different ways:

- **Observation.** The business watches customers to see how they behave when purchasing (or choosing not to purchase) specific products or services. This is a qualitative method of gathering data. This method is time consuming and costly, but can reveal customer views and feelings about a product that other methods cannot.

**Quantitative data**
Involve the use of numbers such as the size of the market, the growth of the market or the number of customers a business has.

**Qualitative data** Look at views and opinions, but do not provide statistically reliable information.

**Primary market research** Data are gathered first hand. The research is specifically designed and carried out for a specific business.

**Knowledge check 21**

Explain how Walkers Snack Foods, famous for its range of crisps, might use market research if it decided to launch its first chocolate bar.

- **Online surveys.** An ICT method of asking customers questions about a product or service through the use of a range of websites such as social media or a specific question and answer website. Online surveys are widely used by businesses as a way of capturing the views of existing and potential customers and have the added benefit of automatically feeding the results into a database that can collect all the answers. It is a quantitative research method. However, they have low response rates from potential customers so can give a distorted picture of consumer opinion generally.

- **Face-to-face surveys.** Personal interviews are conducted face-to-face to obtain customer views on products or services. It is a costly, but a productive way to get detailed insights from individuals. This method is particularly useful for asking for more emotional response-style questions about a product or service, in which case it would be a qualitative research method.

- **Focus groups.** Groups of potential customers are brought together to discuss their feelings about a product or market. Focus groups are a good way of getting detailed qualitative information about customer tastes and preferences, but again can be expensive compared to other types of methods such as online surveys.

The advantages of a business using primary market research are that it gathers up-to-date views of customers about a product, and questions can be tailored to meet the individual needs of the business.

The disadvantages of using primary market research are that it can be difficult to collect the data, it can take a long time to gather it and it is expensive to carry out. Primary research may provide misleading results if the sample size is not large enough or chosen with care, or if the questionnaire questions are worded so as to bias the answers in a particular direction.

## Secondary market research

Secondary market research uses data already collected by someone else. It has not been designed specifically for the business requiring the information.

Secondary market research can be obtained from a number of sources:

- **Government statistics.** These are available to all businesses and contain data such as demographic trends, for example the rate of rise in the number of under-5s expected over the next five years. This is a quantitative research method. It is free to obtain and usually free from bias. The disadvantages are that the data can be a year or two out of date and all businesses have access to the same information.

- **Mintel and other commercial reports.** Market research reports are available on hundreds of customer products and services. They can provide both quantitative and qualitative data. The advantage of these reports is that they are specifically about a certain market, showing its current businesses and potential areas for new businesses to target their product or services at. The disadvantages are that they are available to any business, they are still not completely focused on specific questions the business might like to know the answers to and they are expensive to buy.

---

**Exam tip**

A risk with market research is that consumers struggle to look into the future. More than 100 years ago Henry Ford said that if he had asked the public, they would have asked for a faster horse rather than a car.

**Sample size** The amount of data collected by a business from customers or potential customers.

**Bias** Where the findings of market research do not give a true reflection of the views of the target audience for the product or service.

**Secondary market research** Data collected by someone else that has not been designed specifically for the business requiring the information.

**Demographic trends** Statistics showing how things are changing within the population, such as age, marital status, place of birth and household income.

- **The business's own data** (e.g. sales figures and the number of customers visiting a business). These quantitative data can be used to help research what customers want from a product or service. The advantage of this research is the business already has the data so it is cheap and confidential. The disadvantage of this research is it may not answer the key questions a business may need to look at to ensure its products or services are successful.
- **A competitor's data** (e.g. publicly available sales and profit figures). These quantitative data can be used to help research how a business is performing in the market compared to another business. The advantages of this research are that it is cheap to obtain and shows rivals' performance in the market. The disadvantages are that every competitor can access it and the information available is very basic so is usually of little real value.

Advantages of a business using secondary market research are that it is time and cost effective because the data already exist and are either freely available or have a lower cost than if the same data were gathered by primary research methods.

Disadvantages of a business using secondary market research are that the business is not gathering its own information, first-hand, it is totally dependent on someone else's efforts and the data may be inaccurate or biased so making business decisions based on them is risky.

## Interpreting and evaluating qualitative and quantitative research

Quantitative research requires sampling that can give results that are typical of the population of customers or potential customers the business wishes to gain data about. For example, the well-respected McKinsey and Company conducted a survey in 2017 about electric car purchases in the USA and used 3,500 people as its sample of the population.

Writing a questionnaire that is also unbiased and meets the objectives of the research is critical to gaining reliable results that a business can make decisions based on. For example, the McKinsey report mentioned who was considering buying an electric car (30%) and who had bought one (3%).

Finally, the research collected has to be valid, i.e. good enough to be relied on as a true representation of the whole population the business is interested in. There are many instances where one of the essential elements of quantitative research is not reliable, creating useless and potentially costly data.

With qualitative research the attitudes and habits of consumers need to be interpreted by those qualified to do this type of work, usually psychologists. The questions asked need to be valid in order to gain responses that are representative of consumers in general.

**Knowledge check 22**

Explain why bias may be a problem in research for a new product launch.

**Exam tip**

Data in the extract should be used to build your arguments about trends, but remember to look at the bigger market picture as well for high marks.

An example of a very costly mistake with quantitative and qualitative market research is that made by Coca-Cola in the 1980s. The company completed 200,000 blind tastings of 'new coke' with more than half of those taking part preferring this to the original coke and Pepsi. As a result, the 'classic' coke was withdrawn with disastrous sales results and 'new coke' was later withdrawn. One of the main reasons for the failure of the research was that the tasters were not asked to decide if they would give up the original coke for 'new coke', creating a bias in the findings.

# Sampling

Sampling is a method of obtaining a representative number of people in order to find out about the whole group.

The population needs to be defined, e.g. Manchester United fans between 16 and 24 years old. Then the sample size needs to be decided on, taking into account:

- the margin of error that is acceptable, e.g. +/−5%. The lower the margin of error the higher the sample size usually is
- the confidence level that is required from the sample, with 95% usually providing strong conclusions

Bias in the chosen sample needs to be reduced as much as possible to ensure that the results are accurate and truly representative of the whole population.

## The difference between quota and random sampling methods

Quota sampling aims to obtain a sample representative of the whole population, dividing it into variables such as age or income. A quota sample is then taken from each variable.

For example, if a business wishes to do market research on how often men and women purchase perfume it would first look at the percentage of women and men that make up the population of the UK. The World Bank stated the figure was 50.7% for women and 49.3% for men in 2015, which means the quota sample should reflect this to ensure the research reflects this split.

Quota sampling is relatively cheap and easy to create and complete. However, it is not random so bias in the results can be a problem.

Random sampling means that each person in the chosen population has an equal chance of being selected. As each person in the population has an equal chance of being chosen the results avoid bias. For example, if a business wants to know what the most popular mobile phone is at your school it will choose a percentage of pupils to ask totally at random.

Random sampling is easy to design, but needs an accurate list of the population, or its results are likely to risk being biased.

**Sampling** A method of obtaining a representative number of people in order to find out about the whole group.

**Quota sampling** This aims to obtain a sample representative of the whole population, dividing it into variables such as age or income. A quota sample is then taken from each variable.

**Random sampling** Each person in the chosen population has an equal chance of being selected.

# Evaluation of the usefulness of sampling for a business and its stakeholders

Table 6 outlines the main advantages and disadvantages of sampling.

**Table 6** Advantages and disadvantages of sampling

| Advantages of sampling | Disadvantages of sampling |
| --- | --- |
| Low cost as only a small proportion of the population has to be researched. These low costs can mean more profit for business owners or be passed on as cheaper products to customers. | The chance of bias can mean the conclusions reached are not representative of the entire population, leading to poor business decisions, poor products and losses. |
| Less time consuming as a smaller number of the population need to be surveyed with similar benefits as above. | Selecting a representative sample that produces reliable and accurate results is difficult and complicated. |
| For some populations, it would be almost impossible for a business to conduct research on the whole population, e.g. companies that operate across the globe such as Apple. | The researcher needs subject specific knowledge in sampling in order to avoid making mistakes that lead to bias. |
| The accuracy of the data can be high so long as the sample is chosen carefully and free from bias. | Sampling presumes the sample has the same views as the whole population which is a very simplistic view of human beings that could lead to inaccurate presumptions. |

## Summary

After studying this topic, you should be able to:
- explain what is meant by market research and the value of carrying it out
- distinguish between primary and secondary market research and qualitative and quantitative data
- evaluate the use of market research to a business and its stakeholders
- explain and evaluate the different methods of primary and secondary market research
- interpret and evaluate quantitative and qualitative research
- explain what is meant by sampling and the difference between random and quota sampling methods
- understand the need to avoid bias in market research
- evaluate the usefulness of sampling for a business and its stakeholders

# Business structure

A **private sector business** is owned by individuals. These range from the smallest business, such as a window cleaner, to large multinational companies, such as Toyota, which are owned by individual shareholders. A **public sector organisation** is owned by the government (e.g. the NHS).

## The aims of private sector businesses

An **aim** is the goal a business wants to achieve. This will depend on the **stakeholders** who are involved in the business.

Business aims may include:

- **Survival:** the business wants to ensure its continuing existence. For a new business, this is likely to be a key objective due to the large amount of risk and uncertainty regarding its success, but it can apply to any business.
- **Profit maximisation:** producing a level of output of the product or service which generates the most profit for the business is important.
- **Sales maximisation:** achieving the highest amount of sales revenue is most important (this does not make much business sense, but some companies in the past have worked at 'boosting sales to over £1 billion for the first time' for example).
- **Market share:** the business focuses on capturing as many customers as possible perhaps, like Facebook in its day, with a view to making profits later.
- **Cost efficiency:** the business tries to reduce all its expenses to their lowest possible levels. This should ensure survival even in a toughly competitive market.
- **Employee welfare:** the business tries to ensure the wellbeing and safety of its employees. This is likely to be one among several objectives.
- **Customer satisfaction:** customers' needs and wants are met as much as possible. (Again, this is likely to be one among many objectives.)
- **Social objectives:** the business tries to ensure it has the maximum positive impact on society and/or the environment.

## The aims of the public sector

The aims of the public sector are different from the private sector in that profit is not often seen as something the organisation wishes to achieve. It is often seen as a by-product of a public sector service rather than an outcome that is pursued actively. Funding for the public sector comes from taxation such as council tax (on properties), income tax (on individual incomes) and corporation tax (on company profits).

Features of public sector organisations include:

- **Non-excludability:** the goods and services provided are not simply for those who have paid for them but for any person who needs and/or qualifies for them (e.g. bus passes for over-60s even if they have not paid into the tax system).
- **Non-rivalry:** one consumer using the product or service does not stop other consumers using the same product/service (e.g. all over-60s have a right to a bus pass — there is no maximum number).

**Private sector business** One which is owned by individuals, from the smallest businesses to large multinational companies which are owned by individual shareholders.

**Public sector organisation** One which is owned by the government (e.g. the NHS).

**Stakeholders** Groups or individuals that are affected by and/ or have an interest in the operations and objectives of a business.

### Knowledge check 23

Following BP's oil disaster in the USA in 2010, what objectives may now be of particular importance to the success of the business?

■ **Merit goods:** a product or service is offered to society on the basis of how deserving it is of public finance, rather than based on profit motives (e.g. education).

Some of the aims of the public sector include:

■ Transformation of the economy. This has become much more of an issue since the vote for Brexit in 2016. The UK government is looking at ways to allow businesses to continue to trade freely within the EU and is also actively seeking new trade agreements to provide businesses with improved export markets such as the USA, India and China. This is taking place through a number of public sector organisations such as the Foreign and Commonwealth Office and the Department for Business, Innovation and Skills.
■ Balanced regional development. The Welsh Assembly and UK government agencies offer grants and loans for a variety of business activities, with the aim of sustainable job creation, particularly in areas of deprivation.
■ Providing a range of services for society to maintain and improve people's standards of living, such as schools and healthcare through the NHS and free prescriptions for those living in Wales.
■ To allow people to live safely and securely by providing an army, police and fire service.
■ To regulate markets that the private sector operates in to ensure society as a whole benefits, for example the Competition and Markets Authority is responsible for investigating any business that is operating in a way that restricts trade.

# Evaluation of the roles of the public and private sectors in providing goods and services

Public sector organisations provide essential services that are not fully provided by the private sector. Postal services, radio and television are examples of services that started out as public sector due to their need to introduce new technology to a wide audience.

Public sector organisations also help prevent the exploitation of customers and avoid the duplication of resources. For example, the NHS was formed to ensure that everyone in society gains healthcare regardless of their financial ability to pay. The NHS can benefit from being able to purchase drugs and other health-related services on such a large scale that it can reduce its costs. For example, individual doctors or hospitals would not have the bargaining power of the NHS when looking to purchase beds from a supplier.

The public sector has, in the past, been seen as a way of protecting jobs and key industries. In the 1960s and 1970s huge areas of industry were in the public sector, such as car manufacturers like British Leyland and the whole of the rail network under British Rail. Steel and coal have also been run by the public sector to protect jobs.

**Exam tip**

Profit maximisation is often used as a focus for the 'evaluate' question. Remember profits are needed to grow a business and pay back investors so look at how established the business is to decide how important this objective is compared to others.

However, there has been an increasing move since the 1980s away from the public sector to the private sector, with most industries now privatised and owned by individuals, through companies. This has included all the steel and coal industries, various car manufacturers and since 2013 Royal Mail.

Reasons for this include the fact that state-run businesses become inefficient. There is little incentive to cut costs or provide better service, due to there being little or no competition. The burden on the government of running them is high and selling them to private individuals has raised money. For example, in 2015 the government sold its final stake in Royal Mail to investors meaning it had made £3.3 billion from the sale, which could help pay for things such as the NHS.

However, private companies often put prices up, for example Royal Mail raised the price of a first-class stamp by 2p to 62p after privatisation. Privatisation also often results in jobs cuts, reduced services and poorer access to services for the disadvantaged in society.

# Different private sector business organisations, including not-for-profit organisations

There are a number of ways a business can be set up:

- A **sole trader** is a business with a single owner. It is the easiest method of starting a business and means the entrepreneur makes all the decisions and benefits exclusively from any profits made. However, the owner is responsible personally for all risks and any losses made. In other words, the owner has unlimited liability for any business debts.
- A **partnership** is a business owned by two or more people who share the decision making, risks and profits. The level of risk is lowered by sharing decision making and capital investment in the business between the partners. However, as decision making is shared the business may develop in a way the entrepreneur disagrees with. Like a sole trader, a partnership has unlimited liability.
- A **private limited company** is a business which is a separate legal entity from the entrepreneur and has limited liability. This means there will be shares in the business and the owner can only lose the capital he or she has invested in it. Any further losses have to be borne by those to whom the company owes money. The shares are not traded publicly and the owner can choose who to sell them to. Those holding shares are called shareholders. A private limited company reduces the risk of financial losses to the entrepreneur as there is limited liability. However, the public are able to see various financial statements made by the business and the costs of setting up and running the company are much higher than the other two methods mentioned above.
- A **public limited company** is defined as a business that is able to offer its shares to the public, normally through the stock market. There must be at least two shareholders and there are greater legal requirements to publish accounts than for a private limited company. As a company gets bigger it is likely that it will need access to a large amount of funds to ensure this growth continues. A public limited company can sell many shares and gain a high amount of capital for growth.

**Knowledge check 24**

Why might John Lewis's success as a retailer be down to the fact that the only shareholders are staff who work for the business?

**Exam tip**

Make sure you know the differences between a private and a public limited company and can relate these to the stimulus material. Making a recommendation as to which is the best approach will impress the examiner.

**Stock market** A market where shares are bought and sold by the public.

**Knowledge check 25**

Name one difference between a sole trader and a partnership.

However, the original owner of the business will see his or her ownership diluted by the issuing of shares and will have less say over the way the business continues to operate.

- A **social enterprise** is a business whose aim is to reinvest its profits in the business or community, rather than being driven by the need to maximise profit for shareholders and owners.
- **Charities** are organisations set up to provide help and raise money for those disadvantaged in society, for example, Oxfam fights poverty and its affects in over 90 countries.
- A **cooperative** is a business or organisation run by the people who work for it, or owned by the people who use it. These people share its benefits and profits. The Co-op retail society is an example of a retail cooperative. There can also be marketing or trader co-ops, for example farmers' co-ops. Finally, there can be workers' co-ops of which John Lewis (which owns Waitrose) is a very successful example.
- **Friendly societies** are set up to help members with different issues, such as sickness benefits, life insurance and pensions. Societies such as Shepherds Friendly (established in 1826) offer savings schemes to their members. Friendly societies are run on behalf of their members with any financial gains being given back to the membership, rather than for example shareholders, and they have special tax advantages over banks. However, societies have to follow strict legal rules so cannot invest in higher risk schemes that might make members more money. Some of the benefits offered to members are also discretionary, which means there is no right to receive payment.

## Limited and unlimited liability

Unlimited liability means the personal possessions of the owners of the business are at risk of being seized if the business cannot pay its debts (e.g. a house owned by a sole proprietor).

Limited liability means the personal possessions of the owner are not at risk of being seized if the business cannot pay its debts. The owner is limited to pay only the amount of money invested in shares and nothing else.

## The advantages and disadvantages of choosing different legal structures

Table 7 outlines the main advantages and disadvantages of different legal structures.

**Table 7** Advantages and disadvantages of different legal structures

| Legal structure | Advantages | Disadvantages |
|---|---|---|
| Sole trader | ■ Quick and easy to set up<br>■ Simple to run, with the owner having complete control of decision making<br>■ Minimal form filling/paperwork | ■ Unlimited liability for all the business's debts<br>■ Harder to raise finance as sole traders often have limited money<br>■ Pay more tax than a company<br>■ The business suffers if the owner is ill |

> **Exam tip**
>
> The key business issue is the difference between having or not having limited liability. In the UK, despite the advantages of limited liability, most firms are sole traders or partnerships and therefore have unlimited liability.

**Unlimited liability** The personal possessions of the owners of the business are at risk from being seized if the business cannot pay its debts.

**Limited liability** The personal possessions of the owner are not at risk of being seized if the business cannot pay its debts.

| Legal structure | Advantages | Disadvantages |
|---|---|---|
| Partnerships | ■ Can limit the effects of unlimited liability through a partnership agreement, e.g. some partners may not be legally liable for the debts of the partnership<br>■ Raising finance may be easier due to the number of business owners<br>■ Increased paperwork can be shared between owners<br>■ Partners have full control of the business | ■ The partners have unlimited liability, even if only one partner is responsible for creating a debt<br>■ Decision making is slower as all partners must be consulted<br>■ More business expenses as have to create and stick to a partnership agreement or abide by the Partnership Act |
| Private limited company | ■ The owners of the company/shareholders have limited liability so do not risk their own personal possessions<br>■ Easier to raise finance through the sale of shares or loans from banks<br>■ The business continues to exist as a separate legal person even when ownership of shares changes<br>■ Possible to pay less tax than other forms of business, e.g. sole trader | ■ Some financial information, such as who the directors are and the profits, has to be made available publicly<br>■ There are more expensive procedures to follow than for unlimited liability businesses, e.g. holding an annual general meeting and having accounts that have been checked by an accountant |
| Public limited company | ■ Has the same benefit of limited liability as a private limited company<br>■ A public limited company can advertise shares to the general public and can raise large sums of money<br>■ Public companies gain large media coverage attracting more investment | ■ A public limited company cannot control who buys and sells its shares, meaning the business can be taken over by competitors<br>■ There is a significant increase in the cost of meeting legal obligations, such as more detailed accounts being made available to the public and its shareholders<br>■ Outside investors are able to disagree and change the way the business is run |

# Factors affecting the choice of legal structure of a business

Factors affecting the choice of legal structure of a business include:

■ The type of business being considered (e.g. a window cleaner would not need the formalities of a limited company).

■ If the owner does not wish to expand then operating as a sole trader with less formality may be the best approach.

■ If the business intends to take high risks and use a large amount of borrowed money it may be better to become a limited company as this offers protection to the owner's own assets and may be more effective at raising finance.

■ If the start-up costs of the business are expected to be low then the risks of failure are lower so being a sole trader or partnership may be the best approach.

■ If the owner wishes to ensure that the business can continue regardless of their situation (e.g. illness) then operating as a limited company or partnership may be the best approach.

# The importance and impact of the legal structure of a business on its stakeholders

A stakeholder is a person, group or organisation that has an interest or concern in a business. Stakeholders include shareholders, employees, managers, suppliers, lenders and the community in which the business operates.

■ **Internal stakeholders** are groups within a business, for example owners, workers and shareholders.

■ **External stakeholders** are groups outside a business, for example the community, suppliers, customers and lenders.

For examples of positive impacts a business can have on different stakeholders, please refer to Table 1 on page 9 of this guide. Negative impacts will be the opposite of those listed in Table 1.

Table 8 shows the importance and impact of a business's legal structure on its stakeholders.

**Table 8** The importance and impact of the legal structure for stakeholders

| Legal structure | Impact on stakeholders |
|---|---|
| Sole trader | The owner bears all the risks and earns all the rewards from the business. Stakeholders, such as customers, suppliers and investors, take extra financial risks dealing with a sole trader due to the relatively low level of financial security and unlimited liability. However, there is scope for tailored customer products and services. |
| Partnership | The partners share the burden of running the business, including a greater range of expertise and access to finance. Financial security is less risky than being a sole trader, though there are still risks such as unlimited liability. Customers are able to receive a range of products and services from partners with a greater set of skills than a sole trader may have. |
| Private limited company | The owners/shareholders have limited liability and benefit from greater perceived status by customers, suppliers and investors. This means the business will be able to raise more capital to invest in products or services and employ staff with a range of skills that can lead to healthy growth. The business may have better customer service as a result, though if the business gets into difficulty stakeholders such as suppliers will only be able to pursue the company for any debts and not the owners/shareholders. Shares cannot be sold publicly, thus restricting the business's ability to raise extra finance. |
| Public limited company | The shareholders and management are separated, meaning the business is able to hire experts to run various parts of the organisation. This can lead to the business being more efficient with customers and shareholders benefiting from a mixture of lower cost products and/or higher levels of customer service. The business can sell shares publicly, leading to easier access to large amounts of funds to help with expansion and growth. Shareholders will get less of a say in the way the business is managed and have little control over how much money they receive as a return on their investment. Limited liability means that suppliers and banks cannot pursue anyone other than the business for outstanding debts. Customers may find that a larger business is less flexible in tailoring its products and services to them. |

| Legal structure | Impact on stakeholders |
|---|---|
| Cooperative | Workers and/or customers have a say and stake in how the business performs, which encourages better customer service and more focus on the needs of customers. Profit may not be seen as the most important objective, giving the business the flexibility to cater for the wider needs of employees. Cooperatives such as John Lewis tend to operate as a limited company with the benefits and risks for stakeholders associated with this approach. |

**Knowledge check 26**

Give one benefit of working for John Lewis compared to working for a public limited company that is not a cooperative.

## Summary

After studying this topic, you should be able to:
- explain the difference between the private and public sector, including their different aims
- evaluate the roles of the public and private sector in the provision of goods and services
- explain the legal structure of different private sector business organisations and the advantages and disadvantages for a business
- explain what is meant by limited and unlimited liability
- evaluate the factors affecting the choice of the legal structure of a business
- explain the main features of not-for-profit organisations
- evaluate the importance and impact of the legal structure for stakeholders of a business

# ■ Business location

## Factors that need to be considered when locating a new business

### The type of business

For example, a factory needs to be located near to raw materials, such as steel for cars, while shops need to be close to customers. Being located near raw materials has the **advantage** of reducing transport costs and being able to react more quickly to fluctuations in demand. The **disadvantage** is that the business may have to locate where transporting goods to the customer is much more expensive and time consuming. For example, commercial salmon fishing is often located in remote parts of the Scottish Highlands as this is their native fishing grounds, but has greater costs due to having to build sufficient infrastructure to farm there.

### The proximity to the market

Some businesses need to be located so they can reach customers easily, e.g. a florist needs to have access to the road networks to make quick and easy deliveries. An **advantage** of being close to the market is the business's ability to attract customers and be able to react to changing demand and customer needs quickly. A **disadvantage** is that being located close to the market may mean obtaining goods from suppliers is more time consuming and expensive. For example, the building of a new nuclear power station at Hinkley Point allows electricity to be sent into the national grid for customers, but the materials and expertise to build this have had to be sourced from France and China at an estimated cost of £18 billion.

### Competitors

Businesses need to consider the location of competitors, e.g. petrol stations may wish to be located far apart to ensure little competition. An **advantage** of taking into account the location of competitors is that the market may not become over saturated with businesses competing for the same customers, resulting in potentially higher profits. A **disadvantage** is that the new business may have to locate in less lucrative areas that may not attract the customers the business needs to flourish.

### Availability and cost of labour

Some businesses need to be located near a skilled workforce, e.g. the need for skilled motor engineers for Formula One means businesses need to be located in the Midlands, where many of these engineers are based. An **advantage** is that the greater the availability of labour, the cheaper the cost to the business. A **disadvantage** may be that having access to a skilled workforce may mean being based away from customers, which could increase costs, such as the transportation of finished products.

## Transport links

Businesses that export abroad may need to be located near a port or airport. An **advantage** of being close to transport links is that the costs of obtaining raw materials can be reduced, as can the costs of transporting goods to market. A **disadvantage** is that building costs may be higher as other businesses will also be competing for the same location. Alternatively, the transport links may be some distance away from the market they are intended for, thereby offsetting any cost benefit of good transport links to raw materials.

## Technology

Many businesses now need access to good communications, e.g. traders using eBay need a good internet connection. An **advantage** of having access to technology is that the business is able to access wider markets and offer more innovative ways of engaging with customers, e.g. Amazon's Prime Air drone service being trialled in 2017 with 30-minute delivery times. A **disadvantage** of having access to technology is that competitors will be able to match or even offer better services as they can see what a rival business is offering.

# Evaluating the choice of different locations for a new business

## Supply factors

Supply factors are concerned with **costs** — costs of labour, land and energy. When starting a new business, location is important as it can affect the costs of the business, for example, renting a shop outside the town centre is much cheaper than on the high street. Often new businesses have limited funds so may have to start from home until sufficient revenue is earned to move to a higher cost location that helps with growth and profit. However, small businesses often offer innovative services and rely on the work of the owner to offset a lack of funding.

## Demand factors

Demand factors are concerned with the availability of labour skills, customer convenience, image and the potential to expand.

Location is also important here due to the ability to **gain sales** — an inconvenient location will not attract customers. Some businesses are not as reliant on location as others. For example, Carwow links new car buyers with car dealerships to find the cheapest car deals, but its location is not related to any geographical place. Carwow is based purely online and can be accessed from a mobile or PC anywhere there is internet access. It is the innovative service and ability to offer cheaper car deals that gains sales.

**Image** may also be related to the location of a business, for example, a new shop selling expensive clothes will need to be in a more upmarket and therefore more expensive part of the high street than one selling second-hand clothes. If the new business cannot raise sufficient finance to base its business in an area that matches its desired image the risk of failure increases. However, if a business can offer something novel and innovative this can offset a less image-friendly location. For example, The Body Shop started life in Brighton in a rundown shop with only 25 products. However, the innovation of environmentally-friendly cosmetics and making a lack of money a selling point, for example customers bringing in their own bottles to put products in, more than offset its poor location.

Choice of location for a new business can mean the difference between success and failure, but innovation may well be able to provide sufficient uniqueness to turn any perceived risks into benefits.

## Summary

After studying this topic, you should be able to:

- explain and analyse the factors that need to be considered when locating a new business, in order to meet its needs

- evaluate the choice of different locations for a new business

# Business finance

## Sources of finance available to entrepreneurs and SMEs

**Finance** is the funding required to set up and expand a business. Finance needs to be matched with the short-, medium- and long-term needs of the business. Sources of finance are where entrepreneurs or SMEs can obtain their funds from (see Table 9).

**Table 9** Short-, medium- and long-term methods of finance

|  | Short term (within a year) | Medium term (1 to 5 years) | Long term (5 years onwards) |
|---|---|---|---|
| **Internal sources** | Retained profits Selling assets | Retained profits | Owner's own capital |
| **External sources** | Overdrafts Venture capital Leasing Grants Trade credit | Bank loans Venture capital Crowd funding Leasing Grants | Bank loans Debentures Loans from family and friends Peer-to-peer funding Crowd funding Leasing Grants Share capital |

## Sources of finance and their advantages and disadvantages

### Internal finance

**Internal finance** means funds found from inside a business. Internal finance can be obtained from:

- **Owner's capital.** This is the money or other capital that the person aiming to set up the business may have saved or otherwise come by, for example, money saved in a bank account. The benefit of using the owner's capital is that there are no interest costs compared to a loan and it can be very flexible in how quickly it is paid back. However, the owner may not have any savings or enough money to finance the business and if the business fails all the capital will be lost.
- **Retained profits.** This is the profit kept in the business rather than paid out to its owners (e.g. a limited company may pay shareholders a dividend). A benefit of using retained profits is that it is cheap compared to loans and the business has the flexibility to decide how much is used and when. However, there is an opportunity cost as the owner or shareholders may want the retained profits as their income and it may not be enough money to finance the business.
- **Sales of assets.** Items of property owned by a person or company, regarded as having value, can be sold. A benefit of using the sale of assets is that not only is cash raised (e.g. from selling a van), but also there are no more costs involved in maintaining that asset. However, businesses do not always have any surplus assets to sell and it is a slow process, so may not satisfy the need for finance in the short term.

**Knowledge check 27**

When might a business not be able to use retained profit?

Dividend A sum of money paid by a company to its shareholders out of its profits.

## External finance

**External finance** means funds found from outside a business. External sources of finance include:

- **Family and friends**. The benefits and risks of using this source are similar to the business owner using their own capital. On top of this, family and friends may want a say or stake in the business which means the owner starts to lose independence in decision making and retaining profits.
- **Banks.** They can provide a fixed-term **bank loan** in return for repayment of the amount plus interest.
- **Peer-to-peer funding.** This means lending money to businesses ('peers') without going through a bank or other financial institution, for example, through a website which matches lenders with borrowers (e.g. Zopa). The benefit of this method of finance is that interest rates tend to be much lower than those that banks offer on loans, meaning a cost saving to the business. However, it is more difficult to gain this type of funding as lenders are much more careful about whom they lend to due to the risks of losing their money. This means new businesses in particular will find it difficult to gain any funding this way.
- **Business angels.** These are wealthy, entrepreneurial individuals who provide capital in return for a share in the business, for example shares in a limited company. *Dragon's Den* is a television programme that encourages such finance.
- **Crowd funding** is where the business gains funding by raising small amounts of money from a large number of people, normally via internet sites such as Crowdfunder. A benefit of this source of finance is that smaller investors are more likely to take risks, particularly if the business idea is well marketed and the business can decide what it will give in return for investment. However, this source of finance is much more dependent on the ability of the business to market its idea to investors and if the project fails this may damage the reputation of the business.
- **Other businesses**. The benefits and problems are the same as business angels.

## Evaluating the different sources of finance

- **Loan**. This could be a loan from a bank or family and friends. A benefit of using a bank loan is that the owners are not diluting their shareholdings by bringing new shareholders into the business. However, the business will have to make regular payments to pay back the loan and will have to pay interest on the loan, meaning increased fixed costs.
- **Share capital.** This consists of funds raised by issuing shares in return for cash. This method is only available to a business which is a limited company. The benefit of using share capital is that there are no interest or repayment costs attached to it. However, the problem with share capital is that it is costly and means giving away some of the company and its profits to investors.
- **Venture capital.** This is money invested in a business in which there is a substantial element of risk. An example of a type of investor that would risk venture capital is a business angel. The benefit of getting finance from venture capitalists is that they have money available quickly and can also provide business expertise to help make the investment a success. However, a proportion of the ownership of the business and some

---

**Knowledge check 28**

Which type of business would be particularly suited to crowd funding?

**Exam tip**

You need to be able to identify the most appropriate source of finance for the type of business in the context, making sure you can give reasons for and against its use.

**Share capital** Funds raised by issuing shares in return for cash.

**Venture capital** Money invested in a business in which there is a substantial element of risk.

---

of its profits will need to be given to the investor, meaning a loss of independence in decision making and profits.

- **Overdraft.** This is where a bank allows a firm to take out more money than it has in its bank account. An overdraft can provide very short-term finance for situations where the business is short of cash, for example to pay for raw materials. The benefit of using this method of finance is that it can be used to cover short-term debts. However, the disadvantage is that the bank may ask for repayment at any time and a high level of interest is charged on this type of loan.

- **Leasing.** This is a financial facility allowing a business to use an asset, such as an industrial robot, over a fixed period in return for regular payments. The benefit of using this method of finance is that it allows the business to pay a relatively small amount of money in the short term for an asset, so allowing other funds to be used for other business needs. However, the problem with leasing is that the business does not own the asset so it keeps having to pay for it, month after month.

- **Trade credit.** This is where suppliers deliver goods now and are willing to wait for a number of days before payment, for example 90 days. The benefit is that the business does not have to pay for any goods until some time after they have been delivered, allowing the business to sell on the goods and make a profit. However, the problem with trade credit is that it costs the business to administer the payments and it can only be used for goods supplied rather than for general business expenses or growth.

- **Grant.** This can be given by charities or the government to help businesses get started, especially in areas of high unemployment. A benefit of this method of finance is that the business usually does not have to pay any of the money back and will generally be free to invest it as it feels appropriate. The problem with grants is that they are very difficult to obtain, as many businesses are competing for them, and the criteria for getting a grant can be difficult for a business to meet.

> **Overdrafts** Where a bank allows a firm to take out more money than it has in its bank account.

> **Grant** A sum of money given by a government or other organisation for a particular purpose.

## Exam tip

You need to look at sources of finance in terms of the short, medium and long term when evaluating an extract, especially when completing the 20-mark question.

## Summary

After studying this topic, you should be able to:

- explain and analyse the sources of finance available to entrepreneurs and SMEs
- evaluate the different sources of finance available to entrepreneurs and SMEs

# ■ Business revenue and costs

## The meaning of revenue, costs and profit

### Revenue

**Sales** are when a customer buys a product sold by a business. Sales of the product or services are important to ensure the survival of the business. **Revenue** is the value of sales over a period of time and is calculated as follows:

**revenue** = selling price × sales volume

**Sales volume** is the quantity of product sold in a particular period of time and is calculated as follows:

$$\textbf{sales volume} = \frac{\text{sales revenue}}{\text{selling price}}$$

Sales volume is important to the business to enable it to compare trends over time and gauge how well the product is performing compared with forecasts or budgets.

### Costs

**Costs** are the money a business pays out in order to create and sell its products, for example the cost of raw materials, staff, rent and the interest payable on a bank loan.

Costs can be split into different types:

■ **Fixed costs** are those that do not vary regardless of changes in production or sales levels. They include rent on a factory or office premises, salaries paid to staff, insurance, advertising costs and interest payable on a bank loan.

For example, if a business has a bank loan of £1,000 and the interest paid on the loan is 10% a year then using simple interest the business will have a fixed cost of £100 a year for the interest.

Fixed costs need to be paid by the business regardless of the level of production or sales it achieves. This can be a serious problem when trading is poor, as in a recession.

■ **Direct costs** are those that can be linked to a product or service, for example raw materials.

■ **Indirect costs** cannot be directly linked to a product or service, for example the rent paid for a factory.

■ **Variable costs** are those that change in proportion to the amount of output produced or the amount of products sold. Variable costs include the raw materials used to produce a product, employees' wages if linked to production or sales, energy costs and commission paid to sales staff.

For example, if one employee is paid a piece rate of £10 per item they produce in a factory, and in one week they produce 10 products, then this will cost the business £100. If they work more hours in the second week and produce 20 products then

**Revenue** The value of sales over a period of time.

**Sales volume** The quantity of product sold in a particular period of time.

**Costs** The money a business pays out in order to create and sell its products.

**Variable costs** Costs that change in proportion to the amount of output produced or products sold.

this will cost the business more in wages, £200. Variable costs are important to a business because they can be compared to any forecast made to see if the business is performing as predicted.

■ **Semi-variable costs** are composed of both fixed and variable costs. Costs are fixed to a specific level of production and then become variable after this production level is exceeded. If there is no production then there will still be the fixed cost.

For example, in order to produce a specific number of goods in a factory a certain number of workers are required, which is a fixed cost. If the factory gets a request to increase production due to an increase in demand then the additional wages paid to workers as overtime become a variable cost.

**Total costs** are the total expenses involved in reaching a particular level of production. Total costs can be calculated using the formula:

**total costs** = fixed costs + variable costs

It is important to identify what type of cost a business is paying so that it can be used correctly in the profit and loss account and to be able to analyse the breakeven point for the business. For example, a business may find that variable costs are too high for electricity for a factory and look at reducing these costs by negotiating a lower electricity rate with its energy provider.

# Calculating revenue, costs and profit

## Calculation of revenue

In order to calculate revenue, the following formula should be used:

**revenue** = selling price × sales volume

For example, if Poundland sold 500 items in a day, at £1 each, the revenue would be calculated as follows:

revenue = £1 × 500

revenue = £500

## Calculation of fixed and variable costs

Calculating fixed costs means adding together all identified costs of the business for a period of time. This then produces the business's total fixed costs. The same principle applies to variable costs.

**Table 10** Example of fixed and variable costs of a business

| Month | Output | Fixed costs (£) | Variable costs (£) |
|---|---|---|---|
| January | 10 | 1,000 | 500 |
| February | 10 | 1,000 | 500 |
| March | 10 | 1,000 | 500 |
| April | 15 | 1,000 | 750 |
| May | 20 | 1,000 | 1,000 |
| June | 25 | 1,000 | 1,250 |
| July | 50 | 1,000 | 2,500 |

Table 10 shows the total fixed and variable costs across a period of months, and how they relate to output. For example, a leisure boat-making business may make fewer boats in the winter months as customers are less likely to use a boat due to poor weather. So in January only 10 leisure boats are produced (output) whereas in July production increases significantly to 50. The fixed costs, such as the rent for the factory, do not change as rent does not vary no matter what the level of output. However, the variable costs, such as employees' wages, do vary depending on the level of output. In January, when there is low output fewer hours of work may be required, meaning fewer variable costs, in this case £500. In July, as output increases so do the variable costs — employees will need to work longer hours to produce more boats.

**Exam tip**

Make sure you can calculate fixed, variable and total costs from data given in the exam for 4-mark questions.

## Calculation of semi-variable costs

In the leisure boat business example provided in Table 10, due to the seasonality of the market the factory will vary its output to reflect either anticipated or known demand. In reality it is unlikely that the forecast demand will be sufficiently accurate to anticipate the number of boats actually needed to be built, for example there could be particularly good weather in the summer or perhaps a sporting event might entice more customers to buy boats.

What happens if demand in July is higher than forecast? The £1,000 fixed costs in July may be the maximum capacity of the factory, so if demand requires output to be 100 instead of 50 boats then the fixed costs will actually rise. This is because the business may have to rent premises and machinery for a short time to cover this demand. In this example let us say that the extra fixed costs are £1,500. Associated with this cost will also be extra staff, a variable cost. Let us say that this amounts to another £2,500 in variable costs.

Semi-variable costs would therefore be calculated as follows:

**semi-variable costs** = extra fixed costs + extra variable costs

semi-variable costs = £1,500 + £2,500

semi-variable costs = £4,000

## Profit

**Profit** is the positive gain from an investment or business operation after subtracting all expenses. Profit is important as it can be a source of finance, through retained profit. It can also help a business secure an external source of finance, for example banks can see that a business is able to pay its debts. Profit can be calculated as follows:

**profit** = total revenue − total costs

Table 11 illustrates some simple profit calculations.

**Table 11** A simple calculation of profit

| Total revenue | Total costs | Profit or loss |
|---|---|---|
| £1,000 | £800 | £200 (profit) |
| £800 | £1,000 | (£200) (loss) |
| Total revenue greater than total costs | | Profit |
| Total costs greater than total revenue | | (Loss) |
| Total revenue = total costs | | Breakeven |

## Calculation of gross, operating and net profit

Gross profit is revenue minus the cost to the company of the products or service being sold. Gross profit can be calculated as follows:

**gross profit** = revenue − cost of sales

Gross profit is important because it needs to be high enough to cover the fixed costs of operating and leave some net profit for shareholders. For example, if a business makes £1,000 revenue from selling its products and its cost of selling those products is £800, the gross profit is:

gross profit = £1,000 − £800

gross profit = £200

Operating profit is how much profit has been made in total from the trading activities of the business after deducting other operating expenses such as office salaries, insurance, advertising and energy bills:

**operating profit** = gross profit − other operating expenses

For example, if the gross profit for a business is £200 and the other operating expenses are £50 the operating profit would be:

operating profit = £200 − £50

operating profit = £150

Net profit is what is left after all the costs of a business have been taken from its revenue. This can be calculated as follows:

**net profit** = operating profit − interest

For example, a business has an operating profit of £150 and interest on a loan from the bank of £50 so the net profit would be:

net profit = £150 − £50

net profit = £100

**Gross profit** Revenue minus the cost of selling the products or service.

**Cost of sales** Costs that directly generate the sales, including the cost of raw materials, components, goods bought for resale and direct labour costs.

**Operating profit** Total profit from the business's trading activities before taking account of how the business is financed.

**Net profit** What is left after all the costs of a business have been taken from its revenue.

### Knowledge check 31

If gross profit is £500, cost of sales is £150 and other operating expenses are £300, what is the operating profit?

### Exam tip

You need to be able to compare gross, operating and net profit to evaluate what the figures are saying about the ability of the business to convert sales into profit. Use the extract to work out any problems the business may have, such as high costs of sales.

# Interpret and evaluate the impact of revenue, costs and profit on a business and its stakeholders

Information on revenue, costs and profits is likely to be prepared and evaluated on a very regular basis, particularly by a new business, one that is in financial difficulty or one that is aiming to expand.

**Table 12** Ted Baker plc's 2016 financial statement

| Accounting item | Figure (£ms) | Method of calculation | Comment |
|---|---|---|---|
| Revenue | 456.2 | | The value of all the sales made in the financial year |
| Cost of sales | 183.1 | | The cost of the clothes Ted buys in which can be variable and fixed costs |
| **Gross profit** | **273.1** | Revenue – cost of sales | |
| Fixed overheads (costs) | 213.8 | | Cost of running the stores and head office |
| Operating profit | 59.3 | Gross profit – fixed overheads | |
| Accounting item | Figure (£ms) | Method of calculation | Comment |
| Net financing cost | (0.7) | | |
| Corporation tax | (14.4) | | Unlike some, Ted pays taxes |
| **Profit for the year (net profit)** | **44.2** | Operating profit – financing and tax | |

Looking at the clothing company Ted Baker plc's financial statement in Table 12 we can interpret and evaluate the impact as follows:

- The cost of sales was less than half the money the business made on sales, allowing for a gross profit of £273.1 million. Stakeholders within the business, such as managers and staff, would appear to have sold sufficient products throughout the year through the use of advertising and promotion. Keeping costs as low as possible means more gross profit.
- The cost of sales includes fixed costs, such as contracts with suppliers to make products (e.g. Ted Baker shirts) and variable costs, such as the material needed to create the shirts. Keeping fixed costs low helps reduce the cost of sales, for example working closely with stakeholders such as suppliers to find more cost-effective methods of making shirts.
- Fixed overhead costs are those needed to run the Ted Baker stores and the head office. Keeping these costs as low as possible enables operating profit to be high. This will mean taking advantage of cheaper rentals or purchases of shops and looking at innovative ways to deliver the customer experience with more efficient technology, for example maximising the shop floor space in each store by holding little stock in reserve.

- Corporation tax is the amount the government taxes each company and in 2017 this was 19% of operating profits. The government as a stakeholder wants to create economic conditions for businesses to make higher profits so these can then be taxed in order to pay for the NHS and running of the country in general. Governments need to balance the rate of tax they charge companies with the need to promote new and expanding businesses. Businesses create jobs and wealth, so charging too much tax may discourage companies from expanding — they may perhaps choose to invest in a country with a more favourable tax regime instead.
- For stakeholders such as shareholders and senior managers net profit is very important as the higher this amount the more return on their share investment they may get from the company. Senior managers may also benefit through bonuses, having helped to achieve higher profits. In some cooperatives, such as John Lewis, all staff benefit from higher profits as they each receive a share.
- To evaluate revenue, costs and profit the business, shareholders or other stakeholders should not look at a set of financial results in isolation, such as those shown in Table 12.
- The business should be evaluating its performance on a regular basis, probably daily, to keep costs, revenue and profits in line with expectations.
- Stakeholders can look at trends to see how a business is performing compared to previous data, normally the previous 12 months.
- For example, Ted Baker's revenue in 2015 was £387m which is lower than the £456.2m in 2016, showing a big improvement. Cost of sales was higher in 2016 but this can be expected as the more clothing Ted Baker sells the more it has to buy from suppliers. Operating profits had improved significantly compared to the 2015 figure of £49.7m. This means the business has managed to keep its fixed costs for stores in check while improving its revenue. Net profit for 2016 was also £8.4m higher than 2015, showing a trend of improving results, which benefits shareholders, the government and employees of the business.

# Breakeven and contribution

**Breakeven** is the point at which a business does not make a profit or loss.

**Breakeven analysis** is the study of the revenues and costs of a business at all possible levels of output to establish the dividing point between loss and profit.

Contribution looks at the surplus made on each product sold by the business. It shows how many products need to be sold to cover the fixed operating costs.

# Calculating contribution and understanding its application to breakeven

## Contribution

Contribution can be calculated as follows:

**contribution** = selling price – variable costs per unit

Contribution The difference between sales and variable costs of production.

**Knowledge check 32**

What would happen to contribution if the selling price was raised?

For example, if a travel agent sold holidays to Spain at £200 each, when the variable cost per holiday was £150, the contribution would be:

contribution per holiday = £200 − £150

contribution = £50 per unit

The £50 is how much money is left after deducting the variable costs for each product. This shows us how much surplus is available to cover the company's fixed costs. Once fixed costs have been deducted it then shows us the profit. Knowing contribution helps the business make decisions, especially on pricing.

However, it may be difficult to decide whether the costs are fixed or variable and in the longer term fixed costs could change, reducing the benefit of decisions made on contribution. It also does not show the business whether the products will actually sell.

You may be asked to calculate 'total contribution' using the following calculation:

**total contribution** = contribution per unit × number of units sold

For example, if 80 holidays were sold per week:

total contribution = £50 × 80 holidays sold

total contribution value = £4,000

The business can then establish if it will make any profit by taking fixed costs from the total contribution using the following calculation:

**profit** = total contribution − fixed costs

So, if the travel agent had weekly fixed costs of £2,200

profit = £4,000 − £2,200

profit = £1,800

## Breakeven point

Breakeven point is where the total costs are the same as total revenue. This means that the business makes no profit but makes no loss either. Breakeven point can be expressed as follows:

**breakeven point** = total revenue − total costs

Calculating breakeven point is particularly useful for a new business as it shows the minimum sales target for survival. It can also inform the business as to what the selling price of the product should be in order to break even or make a profit.

The benefits of establishing the breakeven point for the business include being able to predict how long it will take to become profitable, what level of output is required to cover costs and how successful the business is likely to be for potential investors.

## Using contribution to calculate the breakeven point

Contribution can be used to calculate breakeven point using breakeven output. Breakeven output shows the business at what point output matches total costs incurred to make each product. Breakeven output uses the following calculation:

**Exam tip**

If you are asked to work out the volume needed to be sold, give the number of products, not the amount in pounds (or any other currency). This is an easy mark to lose.

**Exam tip**

You may have to evaluate whether contribution is sufficient for the business to be profitable, so make sure you look at the market and financial position of the business as a whole.

**Breakeven point** Where the total costs are the same as total revenue.

$$\text{breakeven output} = \frac{\text{total fixed costs}}{\text{contribution per unit}}$$

For example, the travel agency has fixed costs of £2,200 and the contribution per unit is £50. Breakeven output is calculated as follows:

$$\text{breakeven output} = \frac{£2,200}{£50}$$

breakeven output = 44 holidays

Breakeven output shows the minimum sales required to start making profits. If the travel agency only sells 40 holidays, it will make an overall loss. As shown earlier, sales of 80 holidays provide a substantial profit.

# Construction and interpretation of breakeven charts, including the margin of safety

Breakeven can be shown in the form of a line graph, giving the point where total costs will equal total revenue. The chart will also show at what point the business will make a profit or loss. The number of units sold is plotted on the horizontal (X) axis and total sales, in pounds, on the vertical (Y) axis. The point where the revenue and total costs lines intersect is the breakeven point. This is called a breakeven chart.

## Constructing a breakeven chart

Let us consider a business called Aromatics that wishes to launch a new product at a price of £5 per kg. The fixed costs are £50,000 per year and the variable costs to produce the product are £3 per kg. Aromatics believes the maximum output is 50,000 kg per annum.

To construct a breakeven chart:

1 Draw the vertical axis and the horizontal axis of a graph.

   The vertical axis needs labelling with pounds (£s) at the top and 0 at the bottom. The vertical axis is the costs/revenue. The axis needs to be split using the appropriate scales. In Aromatics' case the maximum amount of output (50,000 kg) will be multiplied by the product price per kg (£5 per kg), giving a maximum value of £250,000. This is shown on Figure 15.

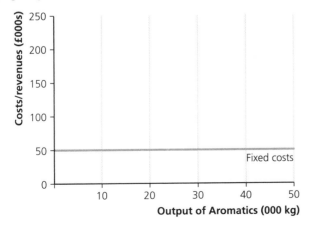

Figure 15 Breakeven chart

Breakeven chart
A graphical representation of total costs and total revenue at all possible levels of output (from zero to maximum capacity).

# Content Guidance

2  Then add the label to the horizontal axis which shows output. This is either the number of sales or the level of production. The axis needs splitting up into appropriate scales and as the maximum output is 50,000 kg this will go at the far side of the axis, as shown in Figure 15.

3  The next stage is to plot a line for the fixed costs. As this amount does not vary regardless of the level of output it is a straight line. In Aromatics' case the fixed costs are £50,000 so the line goes from this cost level straight across, as can be seen in Figure 15.

4  Now a line from the left to the right of the chart needs to be added for the variable costs. For Aromatics the maximum variable costs are:

   £3 per kg x 50,000 maximum output = £150,000

   Make a mark on the chart at this point.

The minimum variable costs will be:

   £3 per kg x 0 minimum output = £0

Make a mark on the chart at this point.

5  Now draw a straight line on the chart from the minimum to the maximum variable costs and add a label. See Figure 16 for a completed example.

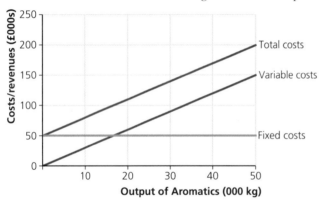

**Figure 16** Breakeven chart

6  Now the variable costs need to be added to the fixed costs to show total costs. The total costs go from the left of the diagram to the right. For Aromatics the maximum total costs are:

   £3 per kg x 50,000 maximum output = £150,000

   £150,000 (variable costs) + £50,000 (fixed costs) = £200,000

Make an appropriate mark on the diagram at this point.

The minimum total costs will be:

   £3 per kg x 0 minimum output = £0

   £0 (variable costs) + £50,000 (fixed costs) = £50,000

Make a mark on the chart at this point. Now draw a straight line between these two points and add a label.

7  The sales revenue now needs to be added to the chart. This is calculated by multiplying the maximum output by the revenue per product. In Aromatics' case the maximum sales revenue is:

50,000 (output) x £5 per kg (revenue per product) = £250,000

The minimum revenue is no revenue:

0 (output) x £5 per kg (revenue per product) = £0

Plot a line from £0 to £250,000 for revenue, as shown in Figure 17.

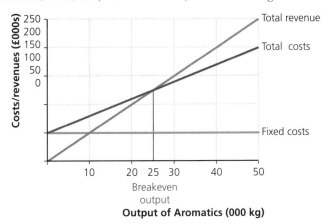

**Output of Aromatics (000 kg)**

**Figure 17** Breakeven chart

The breakeven chart now shows costs and revenue and importantly the point at which the business starts to break even, i.e. the breakeven output as shown in Figure 17. In Aromatics' case the breakeven output is 25,000 kg. A dashed line needs to be drawn, as shown on the chart, to indicate the breakeven output, with a label.

## Margin of safety

Margin of safety is the difference between the actual level of output/sales and the breakeven output. It is like a safety cushion.

Margin of safety shows how much sales can fall before a business reaches its breakeven point. This allows the business to see how much risk is involved at certain levels of output.

For example, if the margin of safety is high, then the business should be safe even if sales prove disappointing. If the margin of safety is low, then a shortfall in the predicted output/sales level can be very damaging. The message to the business is to be as accurate as possible in its prediction of output/sales as this will allow it to take the most appropriate action if problems with breaking even are identified early.

Margin of safety can be calculated as follows:

**margin of safety**    =    current output/sales – breakeven point

For example, for the travel agency considered earlier the breakeven point is 44 holidays with sales currently at 80. The margin of safety is calculated as follows:

margin of safety    =    80 – 44

margin of safety    =    36 units (holidays)

**Margin of safety** The difference between the actual level of output/sales and the breakeven output.

**Knowledge check 33**

Why is a high margin of safety important for luxury goods when inflation is increasing?

**Exam tip**

If you are asked to comment on margin of safety remember that the higher the figure the better — and if the figure is negative the business is making a loss.

## Interpretation of breakeven charts

Figure 18 shows the breakeven chart for Aromatics with the margin of safety indicated.

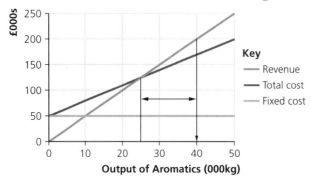

**Figure 18** Breakeven chart showing margin of safety

The key shows the different lines drawn on the chart. Interpretation of the breakeven chart includes:

- Profit can be estimated as the vertical difference between the revenue and total costs line at any point of output.
- The breakeven point is where the revenue and total costs line cross. This is where output is at 25,000 kg.
- Everything below 25,000 kg is produced at a loss, and everything above this is produced at a profit. This is shown by the distance between total revenue and total cost.
- The margin of safety is the difference between the actual level of output/sales and the breakeven output. If sales of Aromatics' products were 40,000 kg at a breakeven output of 25,000 kg the margin of safety is 15,000 kg. The higher the margin of safety, the less risk of making a loss, for example through lower demand for the product. The chart needs to be drawn and labelled as shown in Figure 18 to show the margin of safety.
- Sales of products in reality vary over a week, month and year so the chart needs to have a 'reality check' when considering what may happen to the business.

## Analysis of ('what if') changes in costs and revenue illustrated on a breakeven chart

The breakeven chart can be affected in a number of ways:

- A **price** rise (where the company puts up the product price) will result in a steeper revenue line, meaning breakeven will occur by selling fewer products than at the cheaper price. To construct the revenue line you should adopt the same approach as previously discussed in the Aromatics example. The new revenue line should be dotted and labelled, as shown in Figure 19. The opposite would be the case if the price of the product went down.

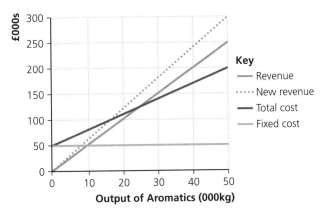

**Figure 19** A rise in price

- A **rise or fall in demand** has no effect on the lines of the breakeven chart. The change simply needs to be read off the chart.
- A **rise in variable costs** will affect both the variable and total cost lines on the breakeven chart. The variable cost line will still start at 0 but the maximum variable cost will be higher. The total cost line will start at the same minimum fixed cost point but again be drawn higher. Calculations are just the same as for the original breakeven chart. Figure 20 shows how the new variable and total costs line should be drawn on the chart — both must be dotted and with labels. The opposite would need to be calculated and drawn on the chart for a fall in variable costs.

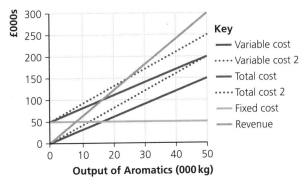

**Figure 20** A rise in variable costs

- A **fall in fixed costs** will cut total costs. This could be due to advances in technology or cheaper building costs. The new fixed costs line will be drawn across the horizontal axis as shown on Figure 21. The new total costs line will be calculated as previously discussed and added to the chart with the correct labels.

**Exam tip**

You may have to interpret and evaluate the figures in a chart in the context of the extract. Try to look at the chart and compare this to what is happening in the wider market to comment on any trends.

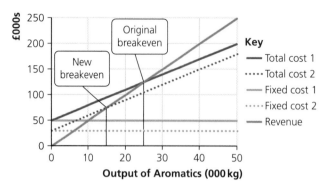

**Figure 21** A fall in fixed costs

# Evaluation of the usefulness of breakeven to a business and its stakeholders

The **benefits** of using breakeven include:

- The business and its investors can perform 'what if' analyses of business objectives such as revenue and variable or fixed costs to establish what sales/output of a product are needed to achieve desired levels of profit.
- The business, senior managers and investors can use breakeven to compare predicted and actual performance and investigate any deviation from expectations, e.g. why total costs are higher than anticipated, such as higher than predicted increases in raw materials.
- The effect on the breakeven point can be considered when looking at rises or falls in the price charged per product and fixed and variable costs. This can help the business target areas of perceived weakness, such as looking for cheaper suppliers to reduce variable costs.
- Stakeholders such as investors or shareholders can hold senior managers accountable when comparing predicted breakeven and actual breakeven.

The **drawbacks** of using breakeven include:

- It may be based on unrealistic assumptions, for example that every item is sold at the same selling price.
- The assumption that sales are the same as output.
- The assumption that variable costs are the same at every level of output (e.g. no bulk buying discounts to benefit from).
- As with all models, breakeven is a simplification of reality — it is fine as a prompt to discussion, but it should not be assumed to be a precise predictor of anything.

**Knowledge check 34**

Why might breakeven analysis be difficult when exchange rates are fluctuating a lot?

**Exam tip**

If the question is assessing the value of breakeven analysis remember that the business must have other data to make decisions on and draw this out in your answer.

## Summary

After studying this topic, you should be able to:

- explain what is meant by revenue, costs and profit, including fixed, variable and total costs to a business
- calculate and interpret revenue, costs and profit and evaluate the impact on the business and its stakeholders
- explain and calculate contribution and breakeven
- construct and interpret breakeven charts, including the margin of safety and the effect of changes in costs and revenue
- analyse how changes in costs and/ or revenue can affect breakeven ('what if' analysis)
- evaluate the usefulness of breakeven to the business and its stakeholders

# Questions & Answers

The questions and answers in this section of the book follow a similar structure to your exams. There are extracts from business situations, data and a selection of all the different types of questions you will be asked to answer either in the WJEC or WJEC Eduqas AS exam or WJEC Eduqas A-level exam.

Immediately below each question there are some examiner tips on how best to approach it (indicated by the icon **e**).

For each question there is both a lower-grade answer (Student A) and an upper-grade answer (Student B). The commentary that follows each answer (indicated by the icon **e**) points out the answer's strengths and weaknesses, and how it could be improved.

## Exam structure

The **WJEC AS** qualification consists of two papers which are worth a total of 140 marks. This guide focuses on Paper 1 which lasts 75 minutes and is worth 60 marks. The paper combines short-answer questions with structured questions. Questions are worth 2, 4, 6, 8, 10 or 12 marks.

The **WJEC Eduqas/WJEC AS** qualification consists of two papers which are worth a total of 130 marks. This guide focuses on Component 1 which lasts 1 hour and is worth 50 marks. The paper has structured questions which are worth 2, 4, 6 or 8 marks.

The **WJEC Eduqas A-level** qualification has three papers which are worth a total of 240 marks. This guide focuses on part of Component 1 which lasts 2 hours 15 minutes and is worth 80 marks. The paper consists of compulsory short-answer question in Section A and compulsory data-response questions in Section B. The paper has structured questions which are worth 2, 3, 4, 6, 8 or 12 marks. This guide will only cover questions related to Business Opportunities. For questions on Business Functions please refer to *WJEC/Eduqas AS/A-level Year 1 Business Student Guide 2: Business functions*, also in this series.

## Exam skills

For the 2-mark questions knowledge of business terms is required. These questions may also ask you to calculate answers using formulae you have learned and data in the extract material.

Questions worth 4 or 6 marks require knowledge of business terms, specific application of the business term from the extract material and an advantage and/or disadvantage of the business term related to the extract material. These questions may also ask you to calculate answers using formulae you have learned and data in the extract material. The examiner will mark this type of question 'from the bottom up'. This means that each mark is earned individually so you will get marks for an advantage, for example, even if you have not provided any context from the extract material. Context is anything unique you discuss from the extract in your answer. It must relate back to the question.

Questions worth 8, 10 or 12 marks require evaluation of the business term using specific evidence from the extract. The safest way to do this is to produce a strong, two-sided argument. You should also aim to make judgements about the business and the key terms discussed, together with proposing solutions to business problems based on the stimulus material and your own business knowledge. The examiner will mark these types of question from a 'best fit' point of view. This means that examiners will give you marks for the highest level of response you show in your answer. For the 8-mark question, to obtain full marks two reasons/factors need to be discussed with a two-sided argument, though the level of detail expected will be less than for the 10- or 12-mark questions. It is worth emphasising the statement at the top level (AO4) of WJEC Eduqas and WJEC mark schemes:

> **Evaluate quantitative and qualitative information to make informed judgements and propose evidence-based solutions to business issues.**

# Technique when evaluating 12-mark questions

As this is the most challenging answer to write on the paper the examiner is looking for some detailed evaluation. To help you gain the highest AO4 marks it may help to consider one or more of the following issues in your evaluation, known as MOPS, which stands for:

- **Market.** What are the characteristics of the market in which the business operates? How do these influence your conclusion? For example, Apple is in the smartphone market which is dynamic and fast changing and therefore requires a lot of money spent on research and development to ensure it keeps its competitive advantage.
- **Objectives.** What are the objectives of the business? How do the business's objectives align to the situation in which it finds itself? How does this influence your conclusion? For example, Apple's objective might be market share, so being the most novel product regardless of the cost may be of greatest importance.
- **Product.** What products or services does the business sell? How might this influence your thinking? For example, Apple may bring out a cheaper iPhone in garish colours to capture more market share.
- **Situation.** What is the current situation the business finds itself in? Does this affect your conclusion? For example, with sales of smartphones peaking Apple needs to find an extension strategy, such as selling to other global markets (e.g. India) to maintain/improve its market share, hence the need for a cheaper phone.

You need to read the extract and the question and use the most appropriate element(s) of MOPS in this context to help look at the wider issues affecting the business that will influence the key issues in the question.

# 1 WJEC AS

## Extract 1

The milk market is worth £2 billion per year in the UK (June 2011). Milk is sold in cheap, clear plastic containers in litres at supermarkets, such as Tesco or Aldi. Typically little attention is paid to the packaging other than the name and type of milk. One litre of milk typically sells for £0.75 across most shops and has a shelf life of 2–3 days.

Cravendale is a highly successful niche brand of milk launched by UK company Arla in 2004. It uses a special type of filtering to remove more impurities from the milk than ordinary milk. Together with white plastic bottles and labels that stand out the milk has a shelf life of up to 3 weeks. Cravendale has a sophisticated marketing campaign using television adverts and social media to raise awareness of its product, spending £5 million on advertising per year. Cravendale is sold in supermarkets at a premium price of £1.15 per litre. Arla posted profits of £8.3 million in 2012.

Tesco has now launched its own brand of filtered milk at the lower price of £0.95 per litre.

## Niche markets

**Briefly explain two drawbacks of operating in a niche market.** (4 marks)

ⓔ 'Briefly explain' means you need to identify drawbacks and how they link to the business, justifying your answer.

Understanding: identify a drawback of operating in a niche market (AO1). This is worth up to 2 marks.

Analysis: understand the impact on the business of each drawback (AO3). This is worth up to 2 marks.

### Student A

A niche market is part of a mass market a. Cravendale milk is a niche market product. b

One disadvantage of Cravendale operating in a niche market is with fewer potential customers compared to a mass market product costs in making the product will be higher. c

ⓔ **2/4 marks awarded.** a The student has mistakenly tried to gain a mark by providing a definition of niche market, even though no marks are available for this. b Although the student used the name 'Cravendale' this is simply restating what the extract text states so gains no mark. c The student gives an accurate drawback for a business that operates in a niche market and so scores 1 AO1 mark. This is briefly developed to gain 1 AO3 mark.

**Student B**

One drawback of Cravendale operating in a niche market is with fewer potential customers compared to a mass market product costs in making the product will be higher. a

Another drawback of a niche market is that successful products, such as Cravendale, are likely to attract more competition. b As Tesco is now in competition with Arla the niche market will become less profitable as there will be comparatively fewer customers to sell to. c

📝 4/4 marks awarded. a The student gives an accurate drawback for a business that operates in a niche market and so scores 1 AO1 mark. This is briefly developed to gain 1 AO3 mark. b The student also gives a further drawback of operating in a niche market for another 1 AO1 mark. c This is briefly developed to gain a further AO3 mark.

This is quite a straightforward question and you should be able to score at least 3 of the 4 marks allocated. For Student A to score only 2 marks (Grade D) shows a lack of preparation and understanding of the skills needed to answer such a question. Student B scores 4 marks (Grade A) simply because he or she had learned some straightforward business theory and had clearly developed their analysis of niche markets. The student has used the short stimulus material to good effect, though this is not necessary to gain full marks here.

**Extract 2**

The milk market has become more sophisticated in recent years, with businesses developing products for the more health conscious consumer and for those looking for a more premium taste. Arla is the market leader in organic milk-based products and has a number of well-known brands such as Cravendale, targeting dads with a £3 million marketing campaign involving the Muppets.

# Market segmentation

**Explain the possible advantages to Arla of using market segmentation.** (6 marks)

📝 The 'explain' command word means you need to show understanding of the business concept 'market segmentation' in terms of its advantages and how this relates to Arla. The question is asking for advantages of market segmentation. The highest skill required is analysis. You should refer to both extracts as they provide the context for this market segmentation question.

AO1: for giving advantages of a business using market segmentation. This is worth a maximum of 2 marks.

AO2: for applying an advantage of market segmentation to Arla's business. You should use application from the context correctly. This is worth up to 2 marks.

AO3: for giving a reason why market segmentation will be an advantage to a business. You should use application correctly to say why market segmentation is an advantage to Arla. This is worth up to 2 marks.

To gain good marks you need to develop two advantages related to the context of the business.

---

**Student A**

Market segmentation involves dividing a market into a smaller set of customers, segments, who have similar needs and interests. **a** Cravendale seeks to meet customer needs by selling milk. **b** One advantage of Cravendale milk using market segmentation is it tries to closely match customer expectations. **c** A disadvantage of market segmentation is that producing a number of different products to suit varied customer tastes is expensive, for example the cost of the Muppets advertising campaign was £3 million. **d**

Another advantage of market segmentation for Arla is that it can take advantage of growth areas in the market, **e** for example the premium milk market. **f**

---

**e 3/6 marks awarded. a** The student gives a precise and accurate definition of market segmentation, but as the question is on advantages of market segmentation this gains no marks. **b** This statement is not a clear advantage of market segmentation so gains no marks. **c** The student identifies an advantage of market segmentation for 1 AO1 mark. **d** The student then gives an accurate disadvantage of market segmentation together with its context. Unfortunately, this does not answer the question so gains no marks. **e** The student correctly identifies a further advantage for 1 AO1 mark. **f** This is then put into context for 1 AO2 mark.

NB: If you can substitute another similar business (e.g. Cadburys) in your answer and it still makes sense your answer will not gain any marks for application to the business context as it is too generic. You need to make your answer unique to the stimulus material to answer this question effectively.

---

**Student B**

One advantage of market segmentation is that separate products can be made for each set of customer needs. **a** This means that Arla can make milk that meets those customers' unique needs with a specialised product, in this case filtered milk. **b** As a consequence of this, Arla can charge higher prices for its products — £1.15 per litre compared to £0.75 for normal milk and make greater sales revenue. **c**

Another advantage is that segmentation can act as a way of growing Arla's profits through specialisation and innovation. **d** As the extract indicates, Arla developed Cravendale in 2004 and has effectively created a niche market with few if any competitors until Tesco recently decided to enter the same segment. **e** This seems to show the success of segmentation as demonstrated by Arla posting £8.3 million profits in 2012. **f**

---

ⓔ 6/6 marks awarded. ⓐ The student has recalled an advantage of market segmentation for 1 AO1 mark. ⓑ Clear use of the extract material is made to show how market segmentation is reflected in Arla's milk product, gaining 1 AO2 mark. ⓒ The advantage is developed with very good use of evidence from the extract, gaining 1 AO3 mark. ⓓ A further advantage is stated, gaining another AO1 mark. ⓔ The advantage is developed with use of the extract for 1 AO2 and 1 AO3 mark. ⓕ The student develops the advantage further using the extract evidence, but gains no further marks as the maximum total has already been reached.

Student A needs to use more context to develop their answer. The student makes assumptions rather than basing their answer on logical interpretation of the extract material, so gaining only a D grade. The student also makes some silly but all too common mistakes, such as discussing disadvantages, which are not part of the question.

Student B makes excellent use of the extract material to make a logical analysis of market segmentation and its benefits to Arla. The final statement gains no marks as the maximum has already been reached, so a student such as this needs to take care to only write enough to gain full marks. If you write more than is needed for an answer you risk running out of time on later questions. Student B uses context very well to gain an A grade answer.

# Income elasticity of demand

**Evaluate the likely impact of an increase in consumer incomes on the demand for milk such as that made by Arla.**

(12 marks)

ⓔ The 'evaluate' command word means you need to supply an extract-based answer with advantages and disadvantages of the business concept. You also need to make a judgement about the business term in the context of the stimulus material and include other relevant business theories. The extract can be used to provide application.

AO2: for good application giving a likely impact on demand in the context of Arla milk. This is worth up to 2 marks.

AO3: for giving good analysis of the likely impacts on demand for Arla milk which should be balanced, detailed, well reasoned and developed. This is worth up to 4 marks.

AO4: for giving excellent evaluation of the likely impacts on demand for Arla milk. The advantages and disadvantages should be balanced and focused on the key issues. Judgements should be made with supporting comments and weight attached to the value of the different points made. This is worth up to 6 marks.

## Questions & Answers

### Student A

Demand is the amount of a good or service which a customer buys at a given price. a Demand for Cravendale milk has been high as it made a profit of £8.3 million in 2012. b One advantage of an increase in consumer incomes is that they will buy more of the product. c This means the demand curve will move to the right and demand will go up, resulting in consumers buying more of Arla's filtered milk. d If consumer incomes go down then the demand curve will shift to the left and demand will go down. e Cravendale milk will make more money if consumer incomes increase. f

**e** **3/12 marks awarded.** a The student has recalled a definition of demand, but as this question contains no marks for knowledge this gains no marks. b The student links the context of Arla's profit in 2012 to demand, but this is a weak assumption and could be due to many other factors so gains no marks. c The advantage is correctly explained in the context of demand and is analysis so gains 1 AO3 mark. d The student attempts to develop the advantage with some context and gains a further AO3 mark and 1 AO2 mark. e The student is not directly answering the question so gains no further mark or higher level. f This is simply an assumption with no development as to why Arla may make more profit and the use of 'Cravendale' is not sufficient to be classed as context as it is not used to answer the question so no more marks or higher level are awarded.

### Student B

One advantage of an increase in consumer incomes is that according to the theory of income elasticity of demand they will buy more Cravendale milk. a This is because Arla's milk is likely to be regarded as a luxury rather than a necessity product as it is more expensive to buy. b This means it is income elastic and therefore customers who normally buy normal milk will switch to Cravendale when they have more disposable income. c A likely impact on Arla is that it will increase its profits from their 2012 levels of £8.3 million. d

However, the increase in Arla's product sales depends on the number of other competitors also operating in this niche market milk. e As the extract states Tesco has also entered the filtered milk market with a similar product to Cravendale but at a lower price of £0.95 per litre. f As a consequence this could be regarded as penetration pricing by Tesco which would have the negative impact on Arla of attracting customers away from its product to Tesco's. g This would mean Arla's profits would not increase as significantly as if it were the only producer of filtered milk. h Arla should reduce its price so it can make more profit and gain market share from Tesco. i

**e** **9/12 marks awarded.** a The student gives an advantage of income elasticity of demand for 1 AO3 mark. b The advantage is explained to suggest that as Cravendale is a luxury product it allows them to charge a premium price. As this includes sufficient context from the stimulus material it is enough to earn 1 AO3 mark and 1 AO2 mark. c The student further develops the impact of incomes rising, relating Cravendale to income elasticity as well for 1 AO3 and 1 AO2 mark. d The student relates this developed point to a likely impact on Arla's profits using context, as well as evaluating the related impact on Tesco as a competitor for 1 AO4 mark. e A potential negative impact regarding the impact of other competitors in the market is introduced but needs further development so gains no further marks. f The student correctly links Tesco as a competitor using the context, but the actual effect is not yet mentioned so no further marks are awarded. g, h The consequence correctly shows the negative impact on Arla, using a potential pricing strategy Tesco may be using with its product, evaluating the impact on both the market segment and Arla's profits for 1 AO3 mark and 2 AO4 marks. i The student attempts to make a judgement as to what Arla might do to reduce the impact of Tesco on its milk sales, but the point is not developed and shows little real link back to the question so gains no further marks.

Student A fails to use the stimulus material to enhance their answer and the advantage they give is very general so fails to gain more than low marks for analysis. Note that the student's fundamental weakness in this answer is poor application to context and evaluation of the key issues so they would only gain a U grade. This could have been a much better answer if the student had used the extract material better.

Student B uses the stimulus material well to give a benefit and risk in context, but rather drifts away from the question in the second part of the answer. The answer also lacks a developed evaluation — it does not look at a greater range of issues surrounding the question. The judgement and recommendation as to what Arla should do lack any development, so the answer only gains low level evaluation marks, but overall it would still be a B grade.

# 2 WJEC Eduqas AS

Rob Law, an entrepreneur, was rejected when he presented his idea for ride - on suitcases for toddlers to *Dragon's Den*, the famous television programme. Ten years later his business has sold 3 million 'Trunkis' and they are the travel case for middle-class parents around the world.

Law has now invented a suitcase for teenagers called the 'Jurni' which is small enough to be airline hand luggage but strong enough to be sat on. It has skateboard wheels, plus it also doubles as a bedside cabinet with special waterproof storage for electronic gadgets, with a retail price of £80. Law says he is marketing the product at 'well off' 13-year-olds. Law puts his success down to determination, persistence and a need to be creative.

The Trunki and Jurni are both developed and sold through Rob Law's company Magmatic Limited of which he has 50% of the shares and which is valued at £13 million. The company has had to spend over £1 million fighting court battles over its rights to its innovative case designs and copies being made in the UK and abroad. This contributed to company losses of £1.4 million in 2015.

Magmatic has traditionally sold products through retailers such as Marks and Spencer but the latest market research suggests selling directly through its own retail outlets could help boost sales dramatically, linking closely with its successful Trunki online shop. This year Magmatic is on track to sell 2 million of its suitcases worldwide. Its products are now stocked in more than 2,500 stores across the UK, as well as in 97 countries. Trunki views China, Japan, Germany, France and India as particular growth markets.

## Entrepreneurial motives

### Identify two entrepreneurial motives.                                                    (2 marks)

ⓔ The 'identify' command word means you need to give a very short example of the business theory questioned.

Knowledge: of entrepreneurial motives (AO1). This is worth up to 2 marks. The extract may give clues to the knowledge needed to gain marks.

**Student A**

An example of an entrepreneur is Rob Law. ⓐ Examples of Rob's entrepreneurial motives are determination, persistence and being creative. ⓑ

ⓔ **0/2 marks awarded.** ⓐ The student has simply given an example of an entrepreneur so no mark awarded. ⓑ The examples of entrepreneurial 'motives' are taken from the extract but as these are characteristics not motives they are incorrect so no marks can be awarded.

**Student B**

Entrepreneurial motives are the reasons that drive a person or people to set up in business. ⓐ Entrepreneurial motives include profit maximisation and satisficing. ⓑ

**2/2 marks awarded.** a The student has correctly recalled a definition of entrepreneurial motives, but as this does not answer the question it gains no marks. b Two examples of entrepreneurial motives are then correctly identified by the student for 2 AO1 marks.

This is a very straightforward question and you should easily be able to score the full 2 marks allocated. For Student A to score 0 marks (Grade U) shows a lack of preparation and understanding of the skills needed to answer the question. Student B shows a lack of understanding as to what the question requires by including a definition, but does then gain both marks for correctly identifying two motives, gaining an A grade.

# Costs

**With reference to Magmatic, why might costs increase?**  (4 marks)

The 'why' command word means your answer must show understanding of the business concept and apply the key issues to the context. This can include a simple definition of costs.

Understanding: defining costs showing good knowledge (AO1). This is worth 2 marks.

Application: using the correct context as directed by the question (AO2). This is worth up to 2 marks.

## Student A

Costs are the money the business pays out in order to create and sell its products. a For example, the cost of raw materials, staff, rent and the interest payable on a bank loan. b

**2/4 marks awarded.** a The student uses the accurate definition of costs, gaining 1 AO1 mark. b The student develops the definition with examples of costs, gaining a further AO1 mark.

## Student B

Costs are the money the business pays out in order to create and sell its products. a Costs can be split up into different types such as fixed costs. Fixed costs are those that do not vary regardless of changes in production or sales levels. b An example of a fixed cost that may increase for Magmatic is the purchase of its own stores. c The market research indicates that renting or buying its own stores could help increase sales and as it has no stores at the moment this would be a large increase in fixed costs, regardless of whether there are sales at the proposed shops or not. d

**4/4 marks awarded.** a The student gives a correct definition of costs for 1 AO1 mark. b The student then develops this definition to identify and define fixed costs for a further AO1 mark. c The student then correctly gives an example of fixed costs in the context of the extract for 1 AO2 mark. d The student then applies a more developed understanding of the fixed costs in the context of Magmatic for a further AO2 mark.

Student A gains only 2 marks (a D grade) by forgetting to apply their understanding of the context of costs to the question. Student B gains 4 marks (an A grade) by not only developing good knowledge of costs but showing a clear understanding of how this applies to the context.

## Importance and impact of the legal structure on stakeholders

**Suggest two stakeholder groups that could be affected by Rob Law's decision to become a private limited company and explain the possible benefits and drawbacks to each stakeholder group.**

(6 marks)

ⓔ The 'suggest' command word means you need to identify two suitable stakeholder groups that could be affected by the decision to become a private limited company. The 'explain' command word means you need to show the benefits and drawbacks to the stakeholder groups chosen, relating them to the context of the business. Using the extract will provide the context for the impact on the stakeholder groups.

AO1: for identifying two suitable stakeholder groups. This is worth a maximum of 2 marks.

AO3: for giving a benefit and drawback of being a private limited company for each stakeholder group chosen. You will have correctly used application of the context and related this to the benefits and drawbacks. This is worth up to 4 marks.

To gain good marks one benefit and one drawback for each stakeholder group needs to be developed, related to the context of the business.

### Student A

Shareholders will be a stakeholder group affected by Rob Law's decision to become a private limited company. ⓐ This is because if Magmatic makes a loss then they will not lose any more money than the cost of their shares in the business. ⓑ A drawback for shareholders is that they do not get to make day-to-day decisions about the business so have little control over its direction. ⓒ

Rob Law is another stakeholder who will be affected by becoming a private limited company. ⓓ As the business is a separate legal entity to Rob if the business makes a loss he does not have to pay any debts out of his own assets, such as the house he might own. ⓔ However, a drawback to Rob is that he does not have full control of the business in terms of making decisions, with other shareholders possibly overriding what Rob may want the company to do. ⓕ

ⓔ **4/6 marks awarded.** ⓐ The student has identified a suitable stakeholder group affected by the choice of being a private limited company for 1 AO1 mark. ⓑⓒ The student attempts to analyse a benefit and a drawback of a private limited company to the stakeholder group, but this lacks both detail and context so gains just 1 AO3 mark. ⓓ A further stakeholder group is identified — though this risks being duplicated with the previous group it still gains 1 AO1 mark. ⓔ The benefit to the stakeholder group is duplicated from the previous example so gains no further mark. ⓕ The student gives a drawback to the stakeholder group which is limited so gains only 1 AO3 mark.

Shareholders. a Magmatic will be able to raise finance for expansion of the sale of the Trunki suitcase into new markets such as China or India, perhaps by Rob selling some of his 50% shareholding. b A drawback for shareholders is that they do not get to make day-to-day decisions about the business so have little control over its direction. c For example, shareholders may not have wished to spend £1 million fighting over rights to exclusively make the cases but have preferred to invest this in expansion. d

Shops that Magmatic supplies to such as Marks and Spencer. e A benefit to retailers who sell the Trunki is that the company has a proven track record having sold 3 million in 10 years so even if Rob Law is no longer running the business as the private limited company is a separate legal entity M&S will still be able to continue being supplied with the products. f This means there will be continuity to revenue. g However, a drawback to stakeholders that are retailers is that private limited companies tend to be run on a small scale so they may not be able to meet surges of demand, as the factory may not be big enough to deliver extra capacity at short notice, leading to lower potential sales. h

e 6/6 marks awarded. a The student has identified a suitable stakeholder group affected by the choice of being a private limited company for 1 AO1 mark. b The student analyses a benefit to the stakeholder using a good level of context for 1 AO3 mark. c d A drawback is discussed in detail with good use of the extract for 1 AO1 mark. e The student is perceptive in choosing a business customer as a stakeholder for 1 AO1 mark. f g The student gives a benefit to customers of a private limited company making good use of the context for 1 AO3 mark. h A drawback is analysed well with context for 1 AO3 mark.

Student A gains 4 marks (a C grade), effectively writing a textbook answer rather than gaining the marks available for using the context to answer the question. The student also takes a risk with potentially overlapping stakeholders. You need to be careful to give two totally unique examples when identifying business issues or marks could easily be lost.

Student B gains 6 marks (an A grade), showing an excellent understanding of the stakeholders and how they may have been affected by private limited company status. This student would just need to be careful with the length of their answer as there is a little more detail than the time allowed for 6 marks requires.

# Demand

**To what extent do you agree with the view that complementary goods might cause the biggest decrease in the demand for Magmatic's suitcases?** (8 marks)

e The 'to what extent' command phrase means you need to look at the evidence that supports and contradicts the argument. It also requires you to explore any alternative views. You need to supply an extract-based answer with fors and againsts of the business concept in the question. The highest skill required is evaluation.

# Questions & Answers

The easiest way to persuade an examiner of your right to earn 8 marks is to write about the factor mentioned in the question and another that will challenge the view. Each sentence should consciously try to hit one assessment objective at a time.

AO1: for giving reasons why demand might decrease due to complementary goods and other key factors. This is worth a maximum of 2 marks.

AO2: for applying the key factors of demand to the business context. This is worth up to 2 marks.

AO4: for giving a reason why demand might decrease and the significance of complementary goods compared to other key factors. Evaluation will be well developed and a judgement may be made on the significance of complementary goods. This is worth up to 4 marks.

## Student A

Complementary goods might cause the biggest decrease in demand for suitcases as they are used for going on holiday. a If families have fewer holidays then they will require fewer suitcases which will decrease the numbers sold and reduce profits. b

However, if the price of the suitcases might go up this may have a bigger impact on a decrease in demand than complementary goods as fewer customers can afford them. c Overall the price of the suitcases will decrease demand more than a decrease in complementary goods. d

---

**e** **4/8 marks awarded.** a The student has demonstrated some understanding of complementary goods though this is not sufficiently developed to gain any marks. b The student develops their point to show understanding of the factor with limited application for 1 AO1 mark and 1 AO2 mark. The student provides general evaluative comments as to why demand may decrease for 1 AO4 mark. c The student shows limited understanding of a second factor that can affect demand, price, gaining 1 AO1 mark. d The student attempts to provide some form of judgement but this is very limited so gains no further marks.

## Student B

For the Trunki suitcase a complementary good would be holidays, so a fall in the demand for holidays would also mean a fall in the demand for suitcases as people only buy suitcases to go on holiday with. a A fall in demand for Trunkis would result in a lower number of cases being sold and make Magmatic look at reducing its prices to compensate for this fall in demand, creating an even bigger loss than the £1.4 million. b

However, it appears that the Jurni suitcase is broadening the appeal of Magmatic suitcases as they can be used for other things, such as a teenager's bedside table. c Demand for holidays is also likely to be negatively affected by a fall in income so it is likely that consumer income would have the greatest decrease on the demand for suitcases, i.e. holidays and Magmatic suitcases can both be classed as luxury goods. ⓓ Looking at the extract Rob Law appears to have decided to reduce the risk of a decrease from a fall in complementary goods due to making the suitcases have more than one use and to be marketed on their uniqueness. ⓔ So long as the suitcases offer customers a unique experience incomes would have to fall significantly before demand starts to suffer for these reasons. ⓕ

ⓔ **8/8 marks awarded.** ⓐ The student has shown a reason why a decrease in demand would take place with limited application to gain 1 AO1 mark and 1 AO2 mark. ⓑ The student has used context to consider the significance of this factor, gaining 1 AO2 mark and 1 AO4 mark. ⓒ A counter argument is used in context to start to evaluate the factor though it gains no marks at this stage. ⓓ The student then considers the relevance of another factor causing a decrease in demand and provides a reason why this might affect demand more than complementary goods in context for 1 AO1 and 1 AO4 mark. ⓔ The student uses the evidence from the extract to evaluate how both factors may affect the business for 1 AO4 mark. ⓕ The student then makes a judgement about the impact of the factors on demand for Magmatic products, together with a recommendation as to what strategy might help the business reduce their effects for a final AO4 mark.

Student A did not develop their answer sufficiently to gain many evaluative marks and also made poor use of the extract, resulting in a D grade answer at best. Student B has written an excellent answer, developing the causes and consequences of a decrease in demand using the extract. The most important point to note is that this type of question requires a discussion of the factor mentioned *and* another factor. You must compare both factors in order to evaluate which is the most significant.

Student B has perceptively shown that income is the most important factor as it affects the complementary good aspect. Do not be afraid to give logical reasons as to why these factors may have little effect on the business, but do back these up with evidence. Try not to use the same context from the stimulus material for each part as this may risk you not gaining any credit for the duplicate context. Overall Student B gives a very good evaluation of the issues to earn an A grade.

# 3 WJEC Eduqas A-level

## Extract 1

Umbro is a globally recognised football brand with a strong heritage derived from more than 70 years' association with the sport of football. Umbro designs, sources and markets football-related apparel, footwear and equipment and its products are sold in over 90 countries worldwide. Based in the UK, the Umbro business was founded in 1924 to supply football strips to local football teams. All products are sourced from independent manufacturers, principally located in the Far East. The brand has lost out in market share in the last few years to Nike and Adidas in lucrative sponsorship deals and has moved into third place as a global brand for football clothing. Umbro has few managers and prefers staff to work independently and creatively to help keep ahead of competitors.

Umbro currently supplies playing and training kit to the Republic of Ireland national team. Umbro and its relevant international licensees supply kit to leading professional clubs worldwide, including PS Eindhoven (the Netherlands), West Ham and Everton (England). The Umbro brand is also endorsed by high-profile individual players, including Real Madrid defender Pepe and Tottenham's Eric Dier.

## Supply

The supply schedule for Umbro trainers manufactured in Taiwan

| Price per pair (£) | Quantity supplied |
|---|---|
| 5 | 20 |
| 10 | 40 |
| 15 | 60 |
| 20 | 80 |
| 25 | 100 |

**In order to try to cut costs Umbro has outsourced its manufacturing of trainers from Taiwan to China. The forecasted saving in production is 10%.**

**Construct a supply diagram to illustrate the impact of Umbro's decision to move manufacturing of trainers to China.** (4 marks)

ⓔ The 'construct' command word means you must complete a diagram from the data and information provided.

Understanding: for correct construction of the supply curve and correctly labelling the axes, price and quantity (AO1). This is worth 2 marks.

Application: for correctly applying knowledge by moving the supply curve to the right and labelling the diagram correctly (AO2). This is worth 2 marks.

Student A

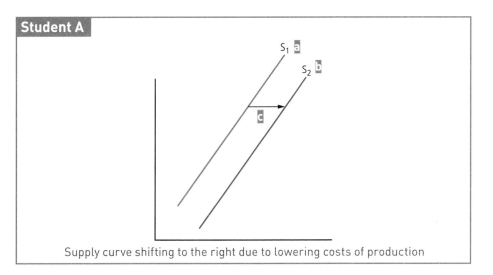

Supply curve shifting to the right due to lowering costs of production

🄔 **2/4 marks awarded.** 🄰 🄱 The student correctly constructs the two supply curves and so gains 1 AO1 mark. 🄲 The student correctly interprets the shift in the supply curve to the right and gains 1 AO2 mark. As the student has added no further labels to the supply curve no additional marks are awarded.

Student B

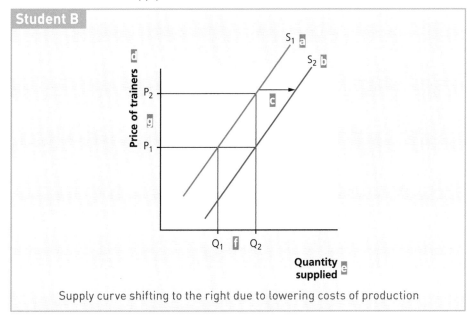

Supply curve shifting to the right due to lowering costs of production

🄔 **4/4 marks awarded.** 🄰 🄱 The student correctly constructs the two supply curves and so gains 1 AO1 mark. 🄲 The student correctly interprets the shift in the supply curve to the right and gains 1 AO2 mark. 🄳 🄴 The student correctly labels the axes price and quantity and gains another AO1 mark. 🄵 🄖 The student correctly draws the effect on price and quantity of a shift in the supply curve to the right and gains another AO2 mark.

Student A draws the two supply curves and correctly labels the shift to the right. The student fails to gain simple marks through failing to label the diagram. The student also fails to gain the analysis mark by failing to draw the effect on price and quantity and so only gains a D grade as a result of some simple omissions.

Student B correctly draws and labels the supply diagram taking into account the extract material which states there is a 10% reduction in the costs of production in China. Labelling of the diagram is important to gain full marks and Student B completes this in full, so gaining an A grade.

# Types of market

**Outline three different types of market.** (6 marks)

ⓔ The 'outline' command word means you need to convey the main points regarding different types of market, placing emphasis on global issues, rather than minute detail. The question is asking you to name different types of market and apply them to the context.

AO1: for naming three different types of market. This is worth a maximum of 3 marks.

AO2: for applying each different type of market to the extract about Umbro. This is worth up to 3 marks.

To gain good marks three different markets need to be identified and related to the context of the business in the extract.

| Student A |
| --- |
| Mass market refers to a large market of customers with widely different backgrounds that a business will not try to distinguish between. ⓐ Umbro operates in a mass market. ⓑ |
| A global market is where goods and services are offered for sale by businesses across different countries. ⓒ Umbro sells globally so operates in a global market. ⓓ |

ⓔ **2/6 marks awarded.** ⓐ The student has identified one type of market for 1 AO1 mark. ⓑ The student attempts to apply the market to the extract but simply makes a statement without any evidence so gains no marks for this. ⓒ The student identifies a further type of market for 1 AO1 mark. ⓓ The student again simply makes a basic statement trying to relate the type of market to Umbro, but provides no evidence so gains no further marks.

NB: If you can substitute another similar business (e.g. Cadburys) in your answer and it still makes sense your answer will not gain any marks for applying it to a business context as it is too generic. You need to make your answer more unique to the stimulus material to answer the question effectively.

Student B

Global market. a. According to the extract Umbro is based in the UK and markets football apparel worldwide in 90 countries so it can be seen to sell products across different countries, a global market. b

Local market. c Umbro started trading in 1924 and sold football strips to local teams such as West Ham, which may have been a short distance from its business premises. d

National market. e Sport retail customers gain a licence to sell Umbro products from the business and then are able to sell to the public in their 'national market' — buyers who are based in the same country. f

e 6/6 marks awarded. a The student has identified a type of market for 1 AO1 mark. b Clear use of the extract material is made to show how Umbro operates in a global market, gaining 1 AO2 mark. c The student has identified a further type of market for 1 AO1 mark. d The extract is used to provide evidence of a local market in context for 1 AO2 mark. e The student has identified a final type of market for 1 AO1 mark. f The student uses the extract to show evidence of a national market for 1 AO2 mark.

Student A needs to use more context to develop their answer and to base their answer on logical interpretation of the extract material rather than making assumptions. They also fail to recognise that this style of question requires three types of market and that there is no credit for definition, so gains only an E grade at best.

Student B understands the needs of the question as they simply identify the markets and then make excellent use of the extract material to show their understanding in context. The student writes a very concise and well explained answer to gain an A* grade answer.

## Extract 2

Internationally, the Umbro group operates principally through a network of 47 licensees who source and distribute products to sports retail customers in their national markets. The group works closely with its international licensees to maintain a global and uniform Umbro brand identity.

The global markets for sports apparel and footwear increasingly overlap with the leisurewear market and Umbro is positioning its range of product lines to benefit from this convergence. Umbro was recently sold by owners Nike to Iconix brand group, who have sports and designer clothing brands.

UK population (000s)

| Age | 1981 | 1991 | 1997 | 2035 |
|---|---|---|---|---|
| 19 or under | 16,337 | 14,800 | 14,970 | 16,892 |
| 20 to 64 | 31,544 | 33,907 | 34,770 | 36,352 |
| 65 plus | 8,472 | 9,099 | 9,269 | 19,956 |
| **Total** | **56,353** | **57,806** | **59,009** | **73,200** |

# Market share and trends

**Umbro is considering developing its market share based on population trends in the 16–25 or the 50+ age group.**

**Discuss which market trend may be the best approach to increase market share for Umbro.** (12 marks)

🅔 The 'discuss' command word means you need to review the pros and cons of the business term and/or the given context using the extract material. You should weigh up strengths and weaknesses of arguments and then support a specific judgement forming a recommendation and conclusion.

AO1: for showing understanding of market share, a definition or some knowledge of trends. This is worth a maximum of 2 marks.

AO2: for good application regarding market share in the context of Umbro. This is worth up to 2 marks.

AO3: for good analysis of the likely impacts on market share for Umbro which should be detailed, well reasoned and developed. This is worth up to 4 marks.

AO4: for excellent evaluation of the likely impacts on market share of targeting market share in the two age groups. The advantages and disadvantages are well balanced and focused on the effectiveness of concentrating efforts on each age group. Judgements will be made with supporting arguments and weight attached to the value of points made. An overall judgement may highlight the best approach for Umbro. This is worth up to 4 marks.

Using the data provided is particularly important for gaining a high mark in this question as they shows trends.

---

**Student A**

Market share is the proportion of sales a business or product has achieved expressed as a percentage in a period of time. 🅐 Market trends means taking a series of market data over a period of time to try to predict what will happen in the future. 🅑 In the extract the population in the UK is increasing and there is forecast to be more people aged 65 and over. 🅒 As people are becoming more active this means that Umbro may be able to make sports clothing that meets the needs of this type of customer. 🅓 As a consequence this may give Umbro a competitive advantage over other businesses such as Nike and gain market share and more profits from this segment of the market. 🅔

However, the problem with market trends is that the information is available to all businesses as it is secondary market research. 🅕 The implication to Umbro is that Nike and Adidas will also know that those aged 50 and above will be increasing in number up to 2035. 🅖 This means that as all businesses in this market have the same access to the data it will depend on how quickly Umbro acts compared to Adidas as to whether it has any competitive advantage in launching sports equipment aimed at the new age group. 🅗 As Nike and Adidas are the market leaders and Umbro appears to have lost some of its competitive edge it is more likely it will gain the competitive advantage with making sportswear for this age group, risking losing market share and ultimately profits. ▯

In conclusion Umbro will need to make sure it uses the market trends data before Adidas and Nike if it is to gain any market share in meeting the needs of the new market segment of older customers and in the longer-term profits. ▯

**🅔 8/12 marks awarded.** 🄰 The student gives a definition of market share, gaining 1 AO1 mark. 🄱 The student then explains what market trends means to gain a further AO1 mark. 🄲-🄴 The benefit of trying to gain market share from the market trend in people aged 65 and over is developed using context and other business terms to answer the question both in terms of market trends and market, gaining 1 AO2 mark and 1 AO3 mark. 🄵 A problem with market trends is given but has little development and no context, so gains no further mark. 🄶-🄸 The student develops the problem with demographic trends with context and by relating it to the issue of market share, gaining 1 AO2 mark, 1 AO3 mark and 1 AO4 mark. 🄹 The student attempts to provide a judgement and recommendation, but as this has little supporting evidence and is undeveloped it only gains 1 AO4 mark.

### Student B

Market trends in this case are based on indicated changes in population size and structure over time in order for a business to try to predict what will happen in the future. 🄰 In this case, the trend indicated in the table clearly shows how the UK population is ageing, with a declining amount of individuals in the 19 years and under section. 🄱 These fall from 16,377,000 to 14,970,000 between 1981 and 1997. 🄲 Although, balancing the reduction in younger people, is the growth in the 20–64-year-old and 65 + sector. 🄳 This latter group is growing significantly from 8,472,000 to 9,269,000 by 1997. These trends are set to continue to 2035. 🄴 The implications of these trends for Umbro, which manufactures primarily sportswear, are it appears to face a static market over time. 🄵 This is because the trend for the 64 and underage group is for lower growth in this segment of the population. 🄶 As a consequence, Umbro faces the possibility of static increases in market share if it pursues this approach, particularly due to fierce competition from the likes of Nike and Adidas. 🄷

The 50+ age group includes the 65 years and older group of consumers which appears to be the growth area in the population, with a forecast doubling in size by 2035. 🄸 Umbro may decide to broaden its portfolio of sportswear to tempt older consumers — an age group which is clearly expanding. 🄹 This may help compensate for a decline in its market share in its main target market. 🄺 Umbro may introduce an entirely redesigned range aimed at the more mature end of the market, targeting much older individuals. 🄻 Thus enabling Umbro to appeal to a wider age range of consumers, helping to increase its market share, sales levels and profit levels in the UK. 🄼 However, it would be wrong to assume that Umbro would suffer from a shrinking market based on the trend figures in the table. 🄽 Trends are figures only for population and give no hint to the levels of popularity of football. 🄾 Even if the trends were to be accurate then there is no accounting for the percentage of potential football fans within this age group. 🄿 For example, all-seater stadiums, Sky Television and the growing popularity of women's football seem to be increasing the popularity of the sport, allowing for potential increases in market growth though perhaps not an automatic increase in market share. **q** The extract also makes it clear that Umbro operate in 90 countries, not just the UK. **r** Therefore market share may be easier to obtain in undeveloped markets where perhaps Nike is not yet established. **s** Market trends are useful for assessing the market Umbro is in but Umbro also needs to use other methods of market research such as Mintel reports to avoid the risk of basing decisions on an incomplete picture of the market thus risking market share and profitability. **t** The implications of the above trends for Umbro would depend on external factors such as the social trend of the growing popularity of football outside of its traditional fan-base and whether Umbro can continue to secure lucrative contracts with leading club and national teams. **u**

**e** **12/12 marks awarded.** **a** The student gives a definition of market trends related to population figures, gaining 1 AO3 mark and 1 AO1 mark. **b–e** The student explains the market trends for the two areas Umbro is considering developing, making good use of the extract material and showing good understanding of market trends for 1 AO1 mark and 1 AO2 mark. **f** The student gives an implication for Umbro of the trends in context, but does not relate this specifically enough back to the question so only gains 1 AO2 mark. **g,h** The student then develops the implication in more detail with evaluation in context, gaining 1 AO3 and 1 AO4 mark. **i–k** The student analyses the potential growth market of 65+ consumers' benefits to Umbro over its current target market for 1AO3 and 1 AO4 mark. **l,m** The student shows excellent analysis of the adoption of this new approach in detail and with context for a further AO3 mark. **n–q** The student also evaluates the wider business context and suggests a strategy for Umbro that may reduce the risks when assessing market trends to improve market share for 1 AO4 mark. **r–u** The student evaluates the benefits of market trends in the context of the wider market the business operates in with a judgement and conclusion for a final AO4 mark.

Student A gives a reasonably concise answer in context, but fails to make sufficient arguments to ensure a reasoned judgement and recommendation regarding the whole of the question. The answer effectively misses an evaluation of the 16–25 trend. However, as the student has provided a balanced and evaluated argument regarding the 50+ demographic in terms of profitability it would still earn a C grade.

Student B makes very good use of the data to back up their assessment of trends and their relationship to the two suggested approaches for Umbro. There are clear lines of well-developed arguments for both options and excellent use of the extract and wider business understanding to draw out the strengths and weaknesses of any decisions made based on limited data. The student offers an overall judgement and suggested approach for Umbro to gain an A*. Where the examiner provides data, it is very important to use it in any relevant discussion.

## Knowledge check answers

1 Businesses take time to grow and expand. There are many business failures so few businesses are able to survive and grow to become large. There is also insufficient demand to warrant businesses growing very large so the markets often limit their size.

2 Richard Branson has a number of traits associated with being a good entrepreneur, including self-confidence and a vision of how his ideas will become a success.

3 As the products have not been tested on animals and are made from natural plant extracts many customers feel they are buying products that protect the environment. This encourages customer loyalty and the ability of The Body Shop to sell products at a premium price.

4 A key characteristic for a sports person is resilience as there will be many times in tennis matches when Andy Murray has been defeated but has still fought back to become a champion, a characteristic which Under Armour feels will help sell its products.

5 SMEs may find it difficult to start up in car manufacturing as they would require a significant amount of financial investment to design and build cars. For example, in 2015 Nissan decided to build a new car plant in Sunderland to build the Nissan Juke at a cost of £100 million. There would also be significant barriers to being successful, such as having to build up customer loyalty and sales from scratch.

6 A new entrepreneur can reduce financial barriers by having a clear and well-researched business plan to show the bank that giving them a loan is a good risk as they are highly likely to be able to pay it back.

7 Employees may ask for a pay rise or a share of the profits. A number of businesses such as Tesco have a profit-related pay element for all employees, to try to encourage greater productivity and customer service among staff.

8 The business plan is based on inaccurate assumptions/research of the market and competitors.

9 Government grants are often related to local area issues such as high unemployment or social deprivation. In certain parts of Wales a grant may be available because of high local unemployment, whereas in central London, where employment is high, there is no need to offer such incentives.

10 Consumers are those that use a product. For a games console such as the Switch this is likely to be teenagers who will be asking parents to purchase it on their behalf. If Nintendo targets teenagers with advertising they will be a much more persuasive method of gaining sales of the console.

11 As a water company, such as United Utilities, has effectively no competition from other similar businesses it operates as a monopoly. This means it can technically charge customers what it likes as the service is only available from it and everyone needs water. There is also no market pressure to reduce costs for similar reasons. However, the government regulates water companies for these reasons so in reality costs and the pricing of water are strictly monitored to ensure customers get a fair deal.

12 Many products sold by global businesses cannot be simply sold across several countries without changes reflecting local customs, preferences or laws. For example, even though BMW manufactures the Mini in the UK it will have to produce right-hand and left-hand drive vehicles as people in different countries drive on different sides of the road.

13 It allows Lindt to sell in greater volume while still maintaining a perception of a luxury brand and premium pricing.

14 Market data can only tell a business what happened in the past and may not reflect the market in the future. For example, the Brexit vote and the resulting fluctuations in the exchange rate would not be reflected in past market data.

15 A market segment worth 20% of the total sales of £3.2 million is:

$$1\% = \frac{£3.2 \text{ million}}{100}$$

$1\% = £32,000$

$20\% = 20 \times £32,000$

$20\% = £640,000$

16 Apple has tried to maintain its dominant position in the tablet market by regularly introducing new models that have unique features compared to those of its competitors.

17 One way a mobile phone retailer can minimise the effect of consumer protection legislation on profits is by ensuring goods are advertised accurately and are also safe to sell, thus avoiding costs from returned items.

18 Ford may increase supply of its cars as the robots replacing the workers are new technology that is likely to make production cheaper. The supply curve for Ford will shift to the right indicating greater supply.

19 A business such as Apple can raise prices with little effect on the demand for its product or service.

20 Bread.

21 Test marketing could be used to see if potential customers were happy with its taste and price and changes made before full market launch.

22 The size of the sample for undertaking primary market research may be too small to draw adequate conclusions about how the product should be developed, priced and marketed.

23 Social and ethical objectives will now play a much more important role in the success of BP as customers and the countries where BP digs for oil will need to be reassured that the environment and safety of its operations are taken seriously, above profit.

**24** As staff also have a share in the business they have a greater motivation to ensure that John Lewis meets customer needs as they will share in the success or failure of the business, through potential dividend payments.

**25** A sole trader is a business with one owner whereas a partnership has at least two owners.

**26** As the workers at John Lewis share in the profits the business makes all staff benefit from improving profits, not just more senior managers.

**27** When shareholders or investors want a dividend payment or repayment of their investment.

**28** New business start-ups who find it difficult to gain funding from other sources such as banks.

**29** Amazon will have lower fixed costs than Tesco as it does not have to pay for physical stores, e.g. the costs of building and maintaining them.

**30** Variable costs for a supermarket can be reduced by only ordering stock when it is about to be sold or sourcing stock from cheaper suppliers.

**31** £200

**32** If the selling price was raised, the level of contribution per unit would go up, meaning the business would have a greater amount available to help cover fixed costs.

**33** A high margin of safety for luxury goods is important when inflation is increasing as it is likely that sales may fall as customers have less real income to spend on the business's products.

**34** Breakeven analysis will be difficult if exchange rates are fluctuating a lot because it means the sale price of goods in different markets will go up or down depending on the exchange rate, either making the product cheaper or more expensive to buy, potentially leading to lower sales or demand not being satisfied.

# Index

# Index